# Using Festivals to Engage Young Children

Religious events and cultural celebrations form an important part of societies throughout the world. They are key to social development and understanding, for celebrating diversity, as well as finding common ground. Covering a wide range of festivals from around the world, this book shows practitioners and teachers how they can introduce young children to some of the ideas behind these events and encourage them to have fun, get creative and work together.

Aimed at those working with children aged 3–7, *Using Festivals to Inspire and Engage Young Children* covers a range of cultural celebration by each calendar month, explaining the background to these events, and provides fun and imaginative activities and stories based around each one. Features include:

- a basic outline of each festival;
- a wide range of activities to suit children at different stages in their development;
- development and learning aims at the end of each chapter;
- suggestions for working with parents and links with home;
- top tips for creating your own activities relating to celebrations;
- story models that can be adapted and used to suit different events.

Highly practical, with an emphasis on fun and hands-on learning, this book is a fantastic resource for Early Years practitioners, Primary School teachers and those who want to inspire young children and celebrate the world we live in.

**Alison Davies** is an author of several fiction and non-fiction books, a professional storyteller and a creative practitioner. She writes for a wide selection of magazines, including *Practical Pre-School*, *Nursery World*, *Teaching and Learning* magazine and *Child Education*. Her features have also appeared in the *Times Education Supplement*, the *Sunday Express* parenting section, and various parenting and mother and baby magazines.

# Using Festivals to Inspire and Engage Young Children

## A month-by-month guide

Alison Davies

Routledge
Taylor & Francis Group

LONDON AND NEW YORK

First published 2014
by Routledge
2 Park Square, Milton Park, Abingdon, Oxon OX14 4RN

Simultaneously published in the USA and Canada
by Routledge
711 Third Avenue, New York, NY 10017

*Routledge is an imprint of the Taylor & Francis Group, an informa business*

*British Library Cataloguing in Publication Data*
A catalogue record for this book is available from the British Library

*Library of Congress Cataloging in Publication Data*
A catalog record for this book has been requested

ISBN: 978–0–415–81582–6 (hbk)
ISBN: 978–0–415–81583–3 (pbk)
ISBN: 978–0–203–59766–8 (ebk)

Typeset in Optima
by Swales & Willis Ltd, Exeter, Devon

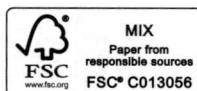

MIX
Paper from
responsible sources
FSC
www.fsc.org   FSC® C013056

Printed and bound in Great Britain by
TJ International Ltd, Padstow, Cornwall

# Contents

# Introduction

## Why use festivals in the Early Years?

Festivals and celebrations have long been used as a way to get groups of people together, united in a common bond, throughout the world. We all like an excuse to celebrate, and particularly with the ones we love. It's human nature to want to feel like we're a part of something; that we belong. Festivals give us that sense of ownership. They give us something to believe in and share, particularly if there's a strong narrative thread to the event. It doesn't matter if it's a spiritual or religious festival, or something more incongruous – the idea is the same. It's about bringing people together, creating a structure that helps us make sense of the world. We can experience each other's cultures, broaden knowledge and learn to empathise and form relationships with others by becoming a part of these events. So it makes sense that they are key to learning, particularly for young children.

This book covers a range of festivals throughout the calendar year, some well known and others more obscure, to give a wide selection of events and practices. Each celebration has something unique to offer, a springboard into learning, from which we can create vibrant and imaginative activities. Most importantly, festivals are fun and the perfect way to engage children and encourage them to connect with each other.

## About this book

Each chapter is dedicated to a month in the year, and highlights some of the major and minor festivals. There's a mix of religious events, and those more cultural celebrations. A basic outline of each celebration is listed, followed by a selection of creative activities that practitioners can use with all ages. Some activities are related to a specific learning and development aim, whilst others cover a number of aims in one go. These are highlighted at the end of each chapter so that practitioners can pick and choose, depending on what they would like to focus on. The idea is to offer a range of activities and ideas for each month. You may not wish to try them all; depending on the groups that you work with, you may have a clear of idea of what you want to achieve. The activities are there as a guide and to show you the potential in these events. They are there to inspire your practice and help you look with new eyes at the world around you. We are all learners. We pick things up every day. We learn from others, and through experience. So by giving children the chance to experience these events, we are giving them key life skills.

Children form a frame of reference based on what they know, so we can use celebrations that already feature in their life as a stepping stone to learning something new. We can take these events and practices and draw similarities with other cultures, thus broadening their understanding of the world. By making it real, we help children form their own opinions, whilst learning valuable lessons in language, literacy, physical and social development.

## Using this book

There is no set way to read this book. Take it month by month, or dip into a chapter at any point. The activities suggested can be adapted, and you may find that you can use them for other things. For example, there are lots of suggestions for story and rhyme starters which could be tweaked to fit in with reading sessions. There are also activities that, although they're linked to a particular celebration, may also fit with a season or time of year, for example, autumn and harvest, which also falls close to the Celtic festival of Samhain.

You may wish to plan ahead, if you've a particular celebration that you would like to cover. Or out of curiosity you could decide to go for something completely different. In most cases, you will find a common celebration amongst some of the more obscure events; this is to give you a starting point, and provide young children with a base from which they can learn.

You may want to let the children take control of their learning and hand the decision over to them. Put all the festivals into a hat, and ask them to pick one out every month. This is a fun way to get them involved and you can use images or symbols for each festival, and make this the starting point by describing what the picture is, and what it might mean. If you're working with older children, you could use this type of activity as a starter activity, by splitting them into groups and getting them to choose a celebration from the hat every month. Each group would then have a specific festival to work on. By using the activities in the book, and any additional ideas that you have, each group would learn about the celebration and share their findings with the other children.

Another idea would be to dedicate a week to all the festivals in this book. Rather than restricting it to each month, you could take your favourites, and split your days to look at each one in turn. If you have a large space to play with, you could dedicate areas around the room to each one, and rotate between them. Or you might decide to go the country route, and link celebrations to places around the world. Again this depends upon the age and level of understanding of the children you are working with.

The key is to show children the importance of celebration, to illustrate through the things that you do, why it's of value. What do we gain from these events? It's not just about distributing information. It's not a history lesson, or the chance to impart religious knowledge. It's so much more. We learn how to value others: how to empathise and understand each other. We learn how to socialise: how to communicate our own opinions. Most importantly, we realise that the best way to learn anything is by having fun, by making the experience real for us, adding a narrative structure to help us fully engage with the notion and using our imagination.

So have fun with this. Be creative. Mix and match ideas and festivals. Be flexible and prepared to learn something new. Go out there and show the younger generation how to celebrate the world we live in. By doing this, you are helping to create individuals who have a sense of pride in themselves and their environment. That's definitely something worth celebrating!

# 1 | January

January, ruled by the Roman god of doorways, Janus, is an important month because it is the first of the year. It is like the first chapter of a book, and indeed it is in this book! You open with so much anticipation and expectancy, not knowing where the story will lead, but hoping for the best. January is a month of optimism, and this should shine through in any learning activity that you undertake. Interestingly, Janus is a god of two faces. One looks back at the past, and the other faces forwards, looking out into the future. This sums up the power of this month and all its festivals. It's a time for new beginnings, a transitional period, where we move from one thing to another. We keep one eye on the past, so that we know where we've come from, but we also look to the future, so that we know where we're headed. Movement is key this month, and each festival listed below represents some kind of movement into a new era or cycle.

## Makar Sankranti

This Hindu festival falls on the 14th of January every year. It marks the beginning of the harvest festival and a time when the days start to grow longer and warmer. It celebrates the journey of the Sun God into the northern hemisphere. The sun is important to Hindus: it represents knowledge, wisdom and light. The idea is that, as the sun travels, we look to the light inside ourselves. We turn away from the darkness and start a new life where we are able to shine brightly and radiate love. This is an auspicious time of year for Hindus and they celebrate this event in many ways, depending on which part of India they live in. Some take a 'holy dip' in one of the rivers to show their respect, and if this isn't possible, they make a point of having a bath on this day. Others prefer to give some kind of offering, including food, clothing, gold and, in particular, pots of sesame seeds. Married women and girls will often apply perfume and sprinkle rose water as a way of appealing to the heavens. Kite flying is also popular at this time of year.

In Southern India, the festival lasts for three days. On the first day they cook up a mixture of rice and milk and offer it to the Rain God; on the second day, they offer the same mixture to the Sun God; and, on the final day, they give their cattle a bath, and dress them up in flowers and bells, as a way of honouring their hard work in the field.

## *Colour carousel*

Think about the ways in which the Hindus celebrate this festival. Split the children into smaller groups. Each group will take an aspect of decoration and have a go at creating something colourful that they can play with. So, for example, one group could have a go at drawing and colouring in kites to fly, while another group could have a go at making paper chains, or flowers which can be worn, carried or waved. Another group might want to take a space in the room and create a river that they can bathe in by using material, or paper painted blue. Have fun and utilise the space you have, and make sure that every corner of the room is filled with colour and movement.

When you're ready, turn this into a carousel of activity. Encourage the groups to move around the room and take it in turns to play with some of the items created. Make the river a game by asking the children to jump in and out and imagine that they are splashing around. Wave the kites in the sky, and count up how many different kinds you have and what colours and patterns have been used. If you have the opportunity you might want to take the group outside to play with their kites.

Take the flowers and do a similar thing, counting up the numbers, looking at the colours used, and thinking about other aspects, like how they might smell and where they might grow. Use this as an opportunity to create a simple rhyme that young children can join in with and use actions to illustrate the words. So, something like, 'The flowers are big, and small and round. I hold them in my hand. The flowers are pink and blue and red. I wave them in the air. The flowers are sweet and light and soft. I throw them everywhere!' Then start again gathering up the flowers, counting as you go, and repeating the rhyme.

## Top tip

With older children, explain the importance of the harvest and the role that the cattle take in ploughing the fields and how this is important to the farmer. Split the children into pairs, so that one child is the farmer and the other child is a cow. The farmers must decorate the cows using the flowers, chains and any other colourful decorations they can find. But to make it interesting and fun, give them a time limit. So count them down and give them a minute to decorate their cow. The most colourful cow wins a prize and is paraded around the room.

# Tu B'Shevat

This is one of the four Jewish new years, known as the New Year for Trees. It's a particularly auspicious time when Jews often eat fruits associated with the Holy Land – grapes, figs, olives, pomegranates and dates. The festival marks the moment when the trees in Israel emerge from their winter sleep.

## *Tree dance*

During this celebration, Jews will often spend time contemplating that 'man is a tree of the field'. Use this phrase as inspiration for an activity based around trees and how they grow. Start by telling the group that they are going to become trees for a day. It's up to them to choose what kind of tree they will be and how they will grow. Start with a simple exercise for all ages. Encourage them to imagine that they are tiny saplings growing beneath the earth. So they might start curled up on the floor and then slowly extend their arms and legs and stretch upwards. Very young children can be helped to stand, or pull themselves up like a tree using chairs and tables. Ask older children to think about how they will grow and move in the breeze and how they will represent branches and leaves. For example, they might draw leaf shapes, colour them in and hold them up, or attach them to twigs to make branches.

Talk about the different types of trees that they could be, so think about fruit trees, oak and ash and ask them to draw pictures of these trees. If it's possible, use this as an opportunity to share some fruit with the group. Grapes are a good choice because they're easy to eat, and you can also use them in counting games.

## *Top tip*

In folklore, particularly old Celtic tales, trees are often associated with nature spirits called dryads. These are a type of fairy spirit that inhabits the tree. Use this as the starting point for a springboard tale, so you might say: 'Once upon a time, there lived a fairy in a tree. Her name was . . .', then get the children to fill in the blanks. 'The fairy had magical powers. She could . . and . . . and . . .', then continue with the rest of the tale. Involve the group by saying. 'One day she heard the sound of someone knocking on the tree, as if they were knocking to come in.' Then get the children to make a tapping sound. 'Who could that be? she wondered. So she opened the door, and standing there was a . . .'

Continue the narrative of the tale, including plenty of opportunities for the group to join in and come up with their own ideas. To finish, you could ask them to have a go at drawing their own fairy spirit, and the tree where he or she lives. Ask them to give their fairy a name, and encourage them to share their work at the end of the session.

# St Basil's Day

St Basil, also known as Basil the Great, was revered for his work with the poor. A good Christian, he worked tirelessly to spread the faith and to help those in need. St Basil's Day, which falls on 1st January, is celebrated in the Greek Orthodox faith. In many homes, a special cake is baked on the eve of the celebration. This cake has a gold or silver coin hidden inside. As part of the festivities, families wait till midnight, turn off all the lights to signify the dawning of the new year, and then exchange hugs and wishes. At this time the cake is cut, with slices going to every family member, including any pets. St Basil also gets a slice, along with an extra-large slice for the poor people of the community. The coin is in one of the slices, and the idea is that whoever receives the coin receives a year of good blessings!

## *Pass the cake!*

The idea of hiding a present inside something is often used in party games like pass the parcel. So why not adapt this traditional activity and give it a 'St Basil' twist. Greek families would often feast on the eve of the new year, so, like them, you're going to throw a tea party. Split into smaller groups and imagine you are setting the table. Think about all the things you will need for this – cups, saucers, plates and a cake. Get everyone to sit in a circle. Set a place for each child, and also set up some imaginary places for pets, friends and anyone who might want to drop by. Make a cake using coloured play dough, and encourage the children to join in with you. Pass the cake around the circle using a rhyming chant, so something like, 'One, two, three, this cake is made for me!' Whoever ends up with the cake at the end of every turn must add something to it. So they might want to make it bigger using another piece of dough, or add a ribbon or some glitter, so that everyone plays a part in building the St Basil cake. This is the reverse of pass the parcel, or discovering a coin inside a cake, because you're building up the layers and giving more, rather than taking anything away – something St Basil would definitely approve of!

## Parent fun

Give out simple cake-making recipes that parents and children can do together. The idea is that they hide a coin in the finished cake. Explain where this tradition comes from, and include some tips for a 'pass the cake'-type party game that can be done at home.

### Top tip

Combine this activity with a special new year's display. This works well with older children, who are starting to understand the concept of a new year and what it might mean. Ask them to think of things that they would like this year to bring. This could be objects like a new bike or a teddy bear, or it could be adventures like a day out at the seaside. Ask them to draw pictures, or bring in items that represent their wishes, then dedicate a corner of the room to this, using a table to display everything. Make your St Basil cake the centrepiece.

## Additional information

The Romans celebrated the new year by paying respect to the great god Janus. They would share figs and dates drizzled in honey, and offer this up in worship to the god. Doors and pathways were sacred to Janus; this is because he looks after those who wish to move on with their life. Statues of Janus show him with two faces to represent the past and future. With this in mind, ask older children to have a go at making masks that they can wear, one looking forwards and the other looking to the past. Talk about the differences. What expressions would they have? Would the forward-looking mask be happy and the backward-looking mask be sad? What kind of colours will they use? Is there a difference in the masks, or are they the same despite the direction they face? Encourage them to swap the masks around and talk about how it makes them feel.

# Development matters covered

Below you will find a list of key development matters covered in the activities above.

## Personal, social and emotional development

*Self-confidence and self-awareness*

30–50 months

- Can select and use activities and resources with help.
- Welcomes and values praise for what they have done.
- Enjoys responsibility of carrying out small tasks.

## Communication and language

### Listening and attention

#### 8–20 months

- Moves whole body to enjoyable sounds, such as music or a regular beat.
- Has a strong exploratory impulse.
- Concentrates intently on an object or activity of own choosing for short periods.

#### 16–26 months

- Listens to and enjoys rhythmic patterns in rhymes and stories.
- Enjoys rhymes and demonstrates listening by trying to join in with actions or vocalisation.

#### 22–36 months

- Listens with interest to the noises adults make when they read stories.
- Shows interest in play with sounds, songs and rhymes.

#### 30–50 months

- Listens to others one to one or in small groups, when conversation interests them.
- Joins in with repeated refrains and anticipates key events and phrases in rhymes and stories.

### Understanding

#### 16–26 months

- Understands simple sentences, e.g. 'Throw the ball.'

#### 30–50 months

- Understands use of objects, e.g. 'What do we use to cut things?'
- Responds to simple instructions, e.g. to get or put away an object.

## 40–60 months

- Able to follow a story without pictures or props.
- Listens and responds to ideas expressed by others in conversation or discussion.

# 🦋 *Physical development*

## *Moving and handling*

### 8–20 months

- Pulls to standing, holding on to furniture or person for support.
- Crawls, bottom shuffles or rolls continuously to move around.
- Walks around furniture lifting one foot and stepping sideways (cruising), and walks with one or both hands held by adult.
- Picks up small objects between thumb and fingers.
- Enjoys the sensory experience of making marks in damp sand, paste or paint.
- Holds pen or crayon using a whole hand (palmar) grasp and makes random marks with different strokes.

### 22–36 months

- Shows control in holding and using jugs to pour, hammers, books and mark-making tools.
- Beginning to use three fingers (tripod grip) to hold writing tools.
- Imitates drawing simple shapes such as circles and lines.

### 30–50 months

- Moves freely and with pleasure and confidence in a range of ways, such as slithering, shuffling, rolling, crawling, walking, running, jumping, skipping, sliding and hopping.
- Draws lines and circles using gross motor movements.
- Uses one-handed tools and equipment, e.g. makes snips in paper with child scissors.

### 40–60 months

- Uses simple tools to effect changes to materials.
- Handles tools, objects, construction and malleable materials safely and with increasing control.

# 📖 *Literacy*

## *Reading*

### 30–50 months

- Enjoys rhyming and rhythmic activities.
- Shows awareness of rhyme and alliteration.
- Listens to and joins in with stories and poems, one to one and also in small groups.
- Joins in with repeated refrains and anticipates key events and phrases in rhymes and stories.
- Beginning to be aware of the way stories are structured.
- Suggests how the story might end.
- Describes main story settings, events and principal characters.

### 40–60 months

- Continues a rhyming string.
- Hears and says the initial sound in words.

# 📦 *Mathematics*

## *Numbers*

### 16–26 months

- Says some counting words randomly.

### 22–36 months

- Recites some number names in sequence.

### 30–50 months

- Uses some number names and number language spontaneously.
- Uses some number names accurately in play.
- Realises not only objects, but anything can be counted, including steps, claps or jumps.

## 40–60 months

- Counts up to three or four objects by saying one number name for each item.

### Shape, space and measure

## 22–36 months

- Notices simple shapes and patterns in pictures.

## 30–50 months

- Shows an interest in shape and space by playing with shapes or making arrangements with objects.

## 40–60 months

- Uses familiar objects and common shapes to create and recreate patterns and build models.

# Understanding the world

### People and communities

## 22–36 months

- In pretend play, imitates everyday actions and events from own family and cultural background, e.g. making and drinking tea.

## 30–50 months

- Shows interest in different occupations and ways of life.
- Knows some of the things that make them unique, and can talk about some of the similarities and differences in relation to friends or family.

### The world

## 30–50 months

- Comments and asks questions about aspects of their familiar world such as the place where they live or the natural world.
- Can talk about some of the things they have observed such as plants, animals, natural and found objects.

### 🎵 *Expressive arts and design*

*Exploring and using media and materials*

#### 8–20 months

- Imitates and improvises actions they have observed, e.g. clapping or waving.
- Begins to move to music, listen to or join in rhymes or songs.
- Notices and is interested in the effects of making movements which leave marks.

#### 22–36 months

- Experiments with blocks, colours and marks.

#### 30–50 months

- Enjoys joining in with dancing and ring games.
- Beginning to move rhythmically.
- Taps out simple repeated rhythms.
- Understands that they can use lines to enclose a space, and then begin to use these shapes to represent objects.
- Uses various construction materials.

*Being imaginative*

#### 16–26 months

- Expresses self through physical action and sound.
- Pretends that one object represents another, especially when objects have characteristics in common.

#### 22–36 months

- Beginning to make-believe by pretending.

#### 30–50 months

- Creates movement in response to music.
- Makes up rhythms.
- Uses available resources to create props to support role-play.
- Captures experiences and responses with a range of media, such as music, dance and paint and other materials or words.

## 40–60 months

- Chooses particular colours to use for a purpose.
- Introduces a storyline or narrative into their play.
- Plays alongside other children who are engaged in the same theme.

Development Matters in the Early Years Foundation Stage (EYFS): © Crown copyright 2012.

# 2 February

Many of the festivals this month have quirky customs and traditions that you can use in creative play. These traditions might have a deeper meaning, which becomes clear as you carry them out. As a society we need rituals to help us make sense of the world. By carrying out a physical action, we show our intent and back it up with the commitment of time and energy. So even the most bizarre rituals have their foundation in something deeper, a need to connect. Sometimes the custom seems far-fetched and unrelated to anything, but there is always a message lurking beneath. This can sometimes become obvious once we perform the ritual. For example, the Celts would clean their homes as part of an Imbolc ritual. The cleaning is not so important as the actual act of clearing things away. It sends a positive message that is linked to purification and preparation for the year ahead. With this in mind, the focus of this chapter is on rituals, the physical act of doing something which then leads us to a deeper understanding of the world.

## Imbolc

This Celtic fire festival was a time to harness the divine energy of the earth to ensure that the harvest would flourish The word itself comes from the Irish word which means 'in the belly'. Imbolc is dedicated to the Celtic goddess of the hearth, Brigid. She was associated with fire, fertility, healing and also poetry. Because of this, many Imbolc rituals centred around the lighting of fires, the idea being that the fire represented the sun's power getting brighter and stronger over the coming months.

Because Imbolc heralds the coming of spring, it's often a time for new beginnings, for cleansing the home and looking to the future. Many pagans today will give their house a good spring clean at this time, in preparation for the year ahead.

This festival is also celebrated by lighting candles and fires, writing and reciting poetry and planting spring flowers. Often houses are decorated with flowers and candles, in particular white candles, as this is the colour most associated with Imbolc.

## Spring magic

There's a freshness about spring, and a feeling of hope and optimism. Share this with the children in your group by dedicating a wall to this season. Start by talking about what spring means to you. What happens during this time of year? Talk about the new shoots coming through, the flowers opening up and the trees growing leaves and blossom. Talk about the animals waking up.

Get the children to pretend they're all flowers in a spring meadow. They've been sleeping during the winter, and they're now emerging from the ground, slowly stretching and bursting open. Play some nice music and talk them through this activity.

Ask them to draw a picture of a spring scene. Encourage older children to talk through this, and explain what they've drawn and why. Display the pictures on the wall. Split the children into groups and ask them to work on larger images of flowers, trees and animals. To give them a starting point you might want to trace the shape on a piece of paper and ask them to decorate it. Finally think about words associated with this month that you can include on your spring mural.

### Top tip

Encourage older children to get poetic, by thinking about rhyming words associated with spring. Start by asking them to put words into pairs that make a nice sound. Give them a starting sentence, something like 'Spring has sprung, oh what fun, see the blue sky and the sun!'

Then ask them what else they might see at this time of year, and encourage them to create rhyming sentences. Once they have a short rhyme that they can repeat, sit in a circle and take it in turns to chant the rhyme. Encourage everyone to join in and think about actions to go with the rhyme.

## Spring board

Create a 'spring' board in the centre of the room. This could be a matted area, or if you have access to a small trampoline, you could use that. The children are going to use this spot to jump up and down, and quite literally spring into spring. Get them to take it in turns and count the number of jumps that they do. Make it a springing competition and see who can do the most. Young

children might need help jumping, but the idea is to get them moving and to encourage older children to use numbers and develop a rhythm.

## Rissun

This Japanese festival, celebrated at the beginning of February, marks the return of spring. It's often called Setsubun, which means the start of any new season.

This celebration is better known as the 'bean-throwing' festival, the idea being that throwing the beans helps to ward off evil spirits. Usually the male of the household will scatter roasted beans, whilst chanting, 'Demons out, good luck in'. In temples and shrines beans are often thrown at the congregation. These are believed to be lucky beans and if you catch them, then you will be blessed with good fortune for the coming year.

### Bean power

Beans are great to play with, and you can have lots of fun throwing them, particularly if you've got a target. Collect some dried beans and lentils and place buckets and pots around the room. Encourage the children to have a go at throwing their beans into the buckets. This is lots of fun, but also messy, so be prepared and ask them to help you gather up the beans afterwards using a sweeping brush or their hands.

Sketch out some patterns on paper, and place on the floor. Now encourage the children to have a go at scattering the beans on these patterns. In effect they're tracing the pictures using the beans.

### Top tip

Older children might like to have a go at creating their own bean pictures by drawing patterns and shapes on to paper, then fixing the beans into place with glue. Encourage them to use other things like buttons or stickers to create a collage or pattern with texture.

## Lent (Ash Wednesday and Shrove Tuesday)

Lent usually falls at some point in February, being the 40 days before the Easter celebration. It starts on Ash Wednesday, and it's a period of contemplation for Christians, who may often fast, or deny themselves something, as a way of observing the 40 days that Jesus spent in the desert. The idea is that, by giving up some vice, they are paying respect to the sacrifice that Jesus made. Shrove Tuesday falls before Ash Wednesday and it's the last chance to feast before the beginning of Lent. It is more commonly known as Pancake Day.

Pancakes are traditionally made as a way of using up fatty foods that would not be eaten at Lent. Pancake racing is thought to have begun by accident in the year 1445. A woman was making pancakes on Shrove Tuesday, but she had run out of time. The church bells rang to signify the start of the service, and the woman, forgetting where she was and what she was doing, ran all the way to the church, carrying her frying pan and wearing an apron!

## Plastercake bake!

Together, have a go at making different-coloured pancakes out of play dough. So shape and flatten them into small circles and pile them up. Next take a dustpan and create a makeshift frying pan. Place the plaster cakes on the dustpan and have a go at flipping them in the air. See how many you can flip at the same time.

Encourage the children to have a go at a mini pancake race across the room. Get them to have a go at flipping whilst they do this!

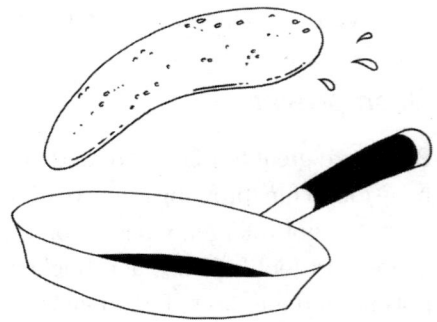

## Pancake man

Use the plaster cakes to illustrate a story about a magical pancake man. Encourage the children to have a go at drawing him. So give him a pancake head and a pancake body, and then ask the children what his arms, legs, eyes, nose and ears might be made out of. Encourage them to think of other sweet treats that could be used, for example, chocolate drop eyes, lumps of jelly for ears.

### Top tip

Older children might like to think about where pancake man lives. Does he live in cake or sweetie land? If so, what is it like there? What are the flowers, trees and houses made of? Who else lives there? Get them to tell a story using pictures and key words to describe a day in the life of pancake man. What would happen if he accidently fell to earth? How would he get back to his own land? How would they help him? Give them plenty of questions as prompts and encourage them to come up with a series of pictures, like a storyboard to explain what happens next. Give them the opportunity at the end of the session to share their stories and ideas, then use them in a pancake man display.

# St Valentine

This lovely festival celebrates all aspects of love. Traditionally it was a celebration of love and fertility and was based around the marriage of the Greek god Zeus to the goddess Hera. Over the years, this has developed with the introduction of the enigmatic St Valentine. The origins of his story are shrouded in mystery, and it's still unclear who he really was. In Ancient Rome, Valentine's Day was part of a bigger festival called Lupercus. This event centred around the fertility god of the same name. The priests at that time would slaughter goats as an offering to the god. They would then run through the streets carrying the skins and touching anybody who crossed their path. This was considered highly fortuitous and young women would go out especially in the hope that they would be touched as they believed it helped with their fertility and ensured easy childbirth.

The real St Valentine was believed to be a priest in Ancient Rome who conducted illegal marriages. At the time the emperor decreed that all marriages should be outlawed, as he was convinced that married men made poor soldiers. St Valentine disagreed, and conducted marriages in secret, because he believed in the power and sanctity of love. He was eventually jailed and beheaded for his crimes. Interestingly, St Valentine had his own love, the daughter of his jailor. It is believed that on the day of his beheading, he passed her a note which read 'from your Valentine'. This is supposedly where the idea of sending cards originates.

## Love hearts

Valentine's Day is the perfect time to introduce young children to card making. Tell them that they're going to make a card for a friend or family member. They might also want to make cards for each other. There's no limit. They can make as many as they like and decorate them using paint, crayons, glitter, stickers, tissue paper and anything else that you might have to hand. With older children, you can encourage them to think about the design and shape of the card. What sort of colours are they going to use and why?

Use a simple rhyme or chant to create a 'kissing song' that the children can recite and put actions to. Something like, 'Kiss kiss, clap clap, wave your hands, tap tap. Kiss kiss, spin around, touch your toes, touch the ground.'

Finally, create a love arch in the centre of the room using building blocks and chairs. This is going to be the kissing spot, and anyone who stands or sits beneath the arch has to recite the kissing song. Encourage pairs and groups to have a go, and take it in turns.

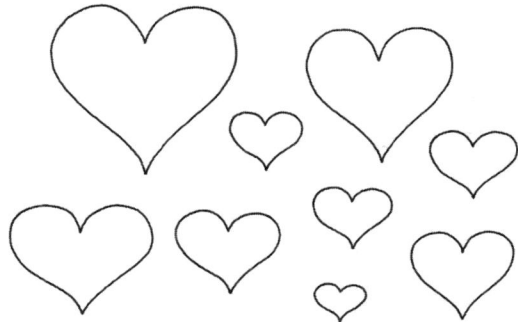

# Development matters covered

Below you will find a list of key development matters covered in the activities above.

## Communication and language

### Listening and attention

#### 16–26 months

- Listens to and enjoys rhythmic patterns in rhymes and stories.
- Enjoys rhymes and demonstrates listening by trying to join in with actions or vocalisation.

#### 22–36 months

- Listens with interest to the noises adults make when they read stories.
- Shows interest in play with sounds, songs and rhymes.

#### 30–50 months

- Listens to others one to one or in small groups, when conversation interests them.
- Joins in with repeated refrains and anticipates key events and phrases in rhymes and stories.

### Understanding

#### 16–26 months

- Understands simple sentences, e.g. 'Throw the ball.'

#### 30–50 months

- Understands use of objects, e.g. 'What do we use to cut things?'
- Responds to simple instructions, e.g. to get or put away an object.

#### 40–60 months

- Able to follow a story without pictures or props.
- Listens and responds to ideas expressed by others in conversation or discussion.

# Physical development

## Moving and handling

### 8–20 months

- Pulls to standing, holding on to furniture or person for support.
- Crawls, bottom shuffles or rolls continuously to move around.
- Picks up small objects between thumb and fingers.
- Enjoys the sensory experience of making marks in damp sand, paste or paint.
- Holds pen or crayon using a whole hand (palmar) grasp and makes random marks with different strokes.

### 22–36 months

- Shows control in holding and using jugs to pour, hammers, books and mark-making tools.
- Squats with steadiness to rest or play with object on the ground, and rises to feet without using hands.
- Climbs confidently and is beginning to pull themselves up on nursery play climbing equipment.
- Beginning to use three fingers (tripod grip) to hold writing tools.
- Imitates drawing simple shapes such as circles and lines.
- May be beginning to show preference for dominant hand.

### 30–50 months

- Moves freely and with pleasure and confidence in a range of ways, such as slithering, shuffling, rolling, crawling, walking, running, jumping, skipping, sliding and hopping.
- Draws lines and circles using gross motor movements.
- Uses one-handed tools and equipment, e.g. makes snips in paper with child scissors.

### 40–60 months

- Uses simple tools to effect changes to materials.
- Handles tools, objects, construction and malleable materials safely and with increasing control.
- Experiments with different ways of moving.
- Jumps off an object and lands appropriately.

## 📖 *Literacy*

### *Reading*

#### 30–50 months

- Enjoys rhyming and rhythmic activities.
- Shows awareness of rhyme and alliteration.
- Listens to and joins in with stories and poems, one to one and also in small groups.
- Joins in with repeated refrains and anticipates key events and phrases in rhymes and stories.

#### 40–60 months

- Continues a rhyming string.
- Hears and says the initial sound in words.

## 🧊 *Mathematics*

### *Shape, space and measure*

#### 16–26 months

- Uses blocks to create their own simple structures and arrangements.
- Enjoys filling and emptying containers.

#### 22–36 months

- Notices simple shapes and patterns in pictures.

#### 30–50 months

- Shows an interest in shape and space by playing with shapes or making arrangements with objects.
- Shows interest in shapes in the environment.
- Uses shapes appropriately for tasks.
- Beginning to talk about the shapes of everyday objects, e.g. 'round' and 'tall'.

## 40–60 months

- Uses familiar objects and common shapes to create and recreate patterns and build models.

# *Understanding the world*

## *People and communities*

### 22–36 months

- Has a sense of own immediate family and relations.

### 30–50 months

- Recognises and describes special times or events for family or friends.

## *The world*

### 16–26 months

- Explores objects by linking together different approaches: shaking, hitting, looking, feeling, tasting, mouthing, pulling, turning and poking.
- Remembers where objects belong.
- Matches parts of objects that fit together, e.g. puts lid on teapot.

### 22–36 months

- Notices detailed features of objects in their environment.

### 30–50 months

- Comments and asks questions about aspects of their familiar world such as the place where they live or the natural world.
- Can talk about some of the things they have observed such as plants, animals, natural and found objects.
- Developing an understanding of growth, decay and changes over time.
- Shows care and concern for living things and the environment.

## 🎵 *Expressive arts and design*

### *Exploring and using media and materials*

#### 8–20 months

- Imitates and improvises actions they have observed, e.g. clapping or waving.
- Begins to move to music, listen to or join in rhymes or songs.
- Notices and is interested in the effects of making movements which leave marks.
- Explores and experiments with a range of media through sensory exploration, and using whole body.
- Moves whole body to enjoyable sounds, such as music or a regular beat.

#### 22–36 months

- Experiments with blocks, colours and marks.
- Creates sounds by banging, shaking, tapping or blowing.

#### 30–50 months

- Enjoys joining in with dancing and ring games.
- Imitates movement in response to music.
- Beginning to be interested in and describe the texture of things.
- Beginning to move rhythmically.
- Taps out simple repeated rhythms.
- Understands that they can use lines to enclose a space, and then begin to use these shapes to represent objects.
- Uses various construction materials.

#### 40–60 months

- Explores what happens when they mix colours.
- Experiments to create different textures.
- Manipulates materials to achieve a planned effect.
- Constructs with a purpose in mind, using a variety of resources.
- Uses simple tools and techniques competently and appropriately.

## Being imaginative

### 16–26 months

- Expresses self through physical action and sound.
- Pretends that one object represents another, especially when objects have characteristics in common.

### 22–36 months

- Beginning to make-believe by pretending.

### 30–50 months

- Creates movement in response to music.
- Makes up rhythms.
- Uses available resources to create props to support role-play.
- Captures experiences and responses with a range of media, such as music, dance and paint and other materials or words.

### 40–60 months

- Chooses particular colours to use for a purpose.
- Plays alongside other children who are engaged in the same theme.
- Creates simple representations of events, people and objects.

Development Matters in the Early Years Foundation Stage (EYFS): © Crown copyright 2012.

# 3 | March

If we think about the word 'march' and the month March, we can see a theme developing. The word 'march' suggests that we walk forward with purpose, it inspires action and growth, and this matches the season perfectly. This is a month of activity and there are many different events and festivals that we can celebrate. The act of marching suggests authority and power, a group of people working together and moving towards a specific destination. With this in mind, I've created activities that will give children the power to make their own decisions, and create a space for themselves. This could be a plot of land for a natural haven where they can embrace the environment, or something more ambitious like a brave and exciting new world where they call the shots. By giving them this responsibility, they learn the value of things and form their own ideas. Let them take the lead, and allow them the space to create something new and exciting!

## St David's Day – 1st March

St David is the patron saint of Wales and the day has been marked as a national festival since the eighteenth century. St David was one of the earliest saints who helped the spread of Christianity throughout the country. It was believed that he came from an aristocratic family and his mother was also a saint. To celebrate this festival, people tend to dress up and wear either a daffodil or a leek; these are both symbols of Wales. Buildings are adorned with flags bearing the Welsh red dragon, and there's usually lots of singing, with choirs gathering and putting on performances. In Primary Schools traditional Welsh costume is often worn, which includes a frilled bonnet and a tall hat, a waistcoat, long wool socks and black shoes. There are often performances which include folk songs, and traditional poetry and dance.

## New world

This activity is something you can do with older children; small children, although they might not understand the meaning of the symbols, can join in by creating pictures. Start by introducing the idea of a symbol for a country, and explain that in Wales they use the daffodil and the leek, and often wear pin badges of these items on St David's Day. Tell the group that they are going to create their own country for the day and give it a symbol to celebrate its existence. Give them space to design the land, by shifting tables and chairs and coming up with a floor plan in the room, so that they can mark out different places in their world, like the enchanted forest, or the lake of mermaids. Ask them what kind of place their country is. Is it a magical land? Are there other creatures that live there? Is it warm or cold? Get them to describe the place. Finally, together come up with a name for the country. Encourage them to think about key words that describe the place and incorporate these into the name.

Split them into four smaller groups, and ask one group to draw some pictures of the world they have created and the different locations. Ask another group to think about a symbol for this new country and to draw it. A third group could look at designing a flag for the country, and finally get the fourth group to draw pictures of some of the creatures that live there.

When all the groups have finished, return to the centre of the room and encourage each group to share their ideas. Create a colourful display of the work around the room, and keep adding to it.

### Top tip

Extend the idea of a new world and encourage older children to come up with stories of their adventures in this place. Start with storyboards, and then use key words and phrases to connect the pictures together. Once they have their story mapped out, encourage them to work together and perform these tales, through a mixture of narration and drama.

# Spring equinox – Ostara

This solar festival celebrates the turn of the seasons and is marked when the length of day and length of night are equal. This happens twice a year, in spring, usually around the 21st of March, and in autumn. The Celts used it as a time to celebrate the coming of spring. They would worship the god and goddess, and their coming together to bear fruit for the rest of the year. Traditionally it's a time for new growth, for the planting of seeds and the creation of new life. Today pagans celebrate Ostara, a name which was adapted to Easter by the Christians, by re-enacting the union of the spring deities. They worship the old Saxon goddess Ēostre, a moon goddess who is linked to fertility and new growth, by carrying out rituals like planting seeds, and decorating the home with flowers. Egg painting is also popular at this time of year, because the egg is linked to Ēostre, as is the symbol of the hare.

## *Natural haven*

As nature is so important at this time of year, and a big part of Ostara celebrations, use this time as an opportunity to get close to the environment. Explain that you're going to create your own magical haven, a mini-garden as part of the spring equinox festivities. If you have some space outside, allocate a plot that you can use to grow flowers and plants. If it's easier, split the children into groups and give them a small plot to design. Get them thinking about the kinds of plants and flowers they want to grow. Encourage them to think about how they're going to make this space special. For example, they might want to decorate it with crystals, stones or ribbons. If you haven't any room outside, you can create pots which you keep indoors and do a similar thing. Once the gardens have been planted, encourage the children to come up with a simple poem for Ostara. Start by asking them to describe a spring scene. Get them thinking about the colours of spring, about plants and flowers, then take it from there and come up with a rhyme that they can repeat and add to. Something like, 'Spring is green, and fresh and clean. Flowers grow, from head to toe. Reaching up into the sun. Hooray, at last, the spring has sprung!'

This catchy rhyme can be repeated in a group, and you can add in actions, by getting the children to imagine they are a flower reaching up towards the sun.

## Parent fun

Take this a step further and encourage the children to create a magical plot at home in their garden. Explain the premise of the idea to parents, and encourage them to make a photographic diary, which charts how the plot is created, and any progress made over the weeks and months.

> ### Top tip
>
> As egg painting is an important ritual, include it in your gardening activities. Get the children to paint eggs which they can use to decorate their plot, or alternatively, they can hide them beneath the soil. They can then take it in turns to find the egg from each other's space, but make sure that they do this before any seeds have been planted, so that you don't disturb their growth.

# Purim

Often referred to as the Jewish Mardi Gras, Purim is a fun festival which celebrates the time when the Jews living in Persia were saved from extermination by a young Jewish woman called Esther. On the eve of Purim families gather together and read the 'Book of Esther'. This practice is repeated the following day, usually in synagogues, when it becomes a colourful affair with lots of raised voices. Those attending dress up and often wear masks; they join in with the story and boo and hiss when the villain of the tale, Haman, appears. The idea is that, by making lots of noise, they are blotting out the name of Haman. During Purim, plays are performed and everyone joins in by playing one of the characters. It's a time for feasting, with lots of merry-making. In certain parts of Israel Purim baskets are made and filled with sweet treats, biscuits and fruit. It is also customary at this time of year to make generous donations to charity.

## Acting up

Select a favourite picture book, and set the scene in your classroom so that the children can perform the tale. Start by creating a stage and thinking about the various items that you might need to do this. Ask the children to think about the different characters in the book. Encourage them to come up with a list of what that character would wear and whether

they need any props. Have some fun with this and get creative with costumes and scenery. Depending on your choice of picture book, you might have to create an entirely different world, like a wood, or a jungle. Give everyone a role to play, so either making things behind the scenes or acting. With younger children, get them involved in sound and movement. So, for example, if your tale is set in a forest, think of the sounds that you might hear, like birds, or the wind howling. If there are other animals in the tale, get them to think about how these animals move and what sort of noises they would make.

## Parent fun

As this is quite an involved activity, it's something you could do over a number of days, so that you work towards a final performance. Get parents involved by suggesting they come along to see it and make it an interactive family event.

### Top tip

With older children, have a go at changing the ending of the tale. So treat the story as a springboard tale. Work towards the point of crisis, the point from which the story could go in any direction, and ask them to storyboard what happens next in groups. Together you can decide upon a different ending, and use this as the basis for your production.

# Development matters covered

Below you will find a list of key development matters covered in the activities above.

## Personal, social and emotional development

### Making relationships

#### 22–36 months

- Interested in others' play and starting to join in.
- Seeks out others to share experiences.

#### 30–50 months

- Can play in a group, extending and elaborating play ideas, e.g. building up a role-play activity with other children.

## *Self-confidence and self-awareness*

### 16–26 months

- Explores new toys and environments, but 'checks in' regularly with familiar adult as and when needed.
- Gradually able to engage in pretend play with toys (supports child in understanding that their own thinking may be different from others').

### 30–50 months

- Can select and use activities and resources with help.

# Communication and language

## *Listening and attention*

### 8–20 months

- Has a strong exploratory impulse.
- Concentrates intently on an object or activity of own choosing for short periods.

### 16–26 months

- Listens to and enjoys rhythmic patterns in rhymes and stories.
- Enjoys rhymes and demonstrates listening by trying to join in with actions or vocalisation.

### 22–36 months

- Listens with interest to the noises adults make when they read stories.
- Shows interest in play with sounds, songs and rhymes.

### 30–50 months

- Listens to others one to one or in small groups, when conversation interests them.
- Joins in with repeated refrains and anticipates key events and phrases in rhymes and stories.
- Is able to follow directions (if not intently focused on own choice of activity).

## Understanding

### 16–26 months

- Understands simple sentences, e.g. 'Throw the ball.'

### 22–36 months

- Understands more complex sentences, e.g. 'Put your toys away and then we'll read a book.'
- Understands 'who', 'what', 'where' in simple questions, e.g. Who's that/who can? What's that? Where is . . .?

### 30–50 months

- Understands use of objects, e.g. 'What do we use to cut things?'
- Responds to simple instructions, e.g. to get or put away an object.
- Beginning to understand 'why' and 'how' questions.

### 40–60 months

- Able to follow a story without pictures or props.
- Listens and responds to ideas expressed by others in conversation or discussion.

## Speaking

### 8–20 months

- Frequently imitates words and sounds.
- Enjoys babbling and increasingly experiments with using sounds and words to communicate for a range of purposes, e.g. teddy, more, no, bye-bye.

### 16–26 months

- Uses different types of everyday words (nouns, verbs and adjectives, e.g. banana, go, sleep, hot).
- Beginning to ask simple questions.

### 22–36 months

- Learns new words very rapidly and is able to use them in communicating.
- Uses gestures, sometimes with limited talk, e.g. reaches toward toy, saying 'I have it'.

- Uses a variety of questions, e.g. what, where, who.
- Uses simple sentences, e.g. 'Mummy gonna work.'

## 30–50 months

- Beginning to use more complex sentences to link thoughts, e.g. using 'and' and 'because'.
- Uses talk to connect ideas, explain what is happening and anticipate what might happen next, recall and relive past experiences.
- Questions why things happen and gives explanations. Asks e.g. who, what, when, how.

## 40–60 months

- Uses language to imagine and recreate roles and experiences in play situations.
- Introduces a storyline or narrative into their play.

## *Physical development*

### *Moving and handling*

## 8–20 months

- Crawls, bottom shuffles or rolls continuously to move around.
- Picks up small objects between thumb and fingers.
- Enjoys the sensory experience of making marks in damp sand, paste or paint.
- Holds pen or crayon using a whole hand (palmar) grasp and makes random marks with different strokes.

## 22–36 months

- Shows control in holding and using jugs to pour, hammers, books and mark-making tools.
- Squats with steadiness to rest or play with object on the ground, and rises to feet without using hands.
- Beginning to use three fingers (tripod grip) to hold writing tools.
- Imitates drawing simple shapes such as circles and lines.

## 30–50 months

- Draws lines and circles using gross motor movements.
- Uses one-handed tools and equipment, e.g. makes snips in paper with child scissors.

## 40–60 months

- Uses simple tools to effect changes to materials.
- Handles tools, objects, construction and malleable materials safely and with increasing control.
- Experiments with different ways of moving.

## 📖 *Literacy*

### *Reading*

### 22–36 months

- Has some favourite stories, rhymes, songs, poems or jingles.
- Repeats words or phrases from familiar stories.

### 30–50 months

- Enjoys rhyming and rhythmic activities.
- Shows awareness of rhyme and alliteration.
- Listens to and joins in with stories and poems, one to one and also in small groups.
- Joins in with repeated refrains and anticipates key events and phrases in rhymes and stories.
- Beginning to be aware of the way stories are structured.
- Suggests how the story might end.
- Listens to stories with increasing attention and recall.
- Describes main story settings, events and principal characters.
- Shows interest in illustrations and print in books and print in the environment.

### 40–60 months

- Uses vocabulary and forms of speech that are increasingly influenced by their experiences of books
- Continues a rhyming string.
- Hears and says the initial sound in words.

*Writing*

## 40–60 months

- Gives meaning to marks they make as they draw, write and paint.
- Begins to break the flow of speech into words.
- Continues a rhyming string.

## Mathematics

*Shape, space and measure*

## 16–26 months

- Uses blocks to create their own simple structures and arrangements.
- Enjoys filling and emptying containers.

## 22–36 months

- Notices simple shapes and patterns in pictures.

## 30–50 months

- Shows an interest in shape and space by playing with shapes or making arrangements with objects.
- Shows interest in shapes in the environment.
- Uses shapes appropriately for tasks.
- Beginning to talk about the shapes of everyday objects, e.g. 'round' and 'tall'.

## 40–60 months

- Uses familiar objects and common shapes to create and recreate patterns and build models.

## Understanding the world

*The world*

## 8–20 months

- Becomes absorbed in combining objects, e.g. banging two objects or placing objects into containers.

## 16–26 months

- Explores objects by linking together different approaches: shaking, hitting, looking, feeling, tasting, mouthing, pulling, turning and poking.
- Remembers where objects belong.
- Matches parts of objects that fit together, e.g. puts lid on teapot.

## 22–36 months

- Notices detailed features of objects in their environment.

## 30–50 months

- Comments and asks questions about aspects of their familiar world such as the place where they live or the natural world.
- Can talk about some of the things they have observed such as plants, animals, natural and found objects.
- Developing an understanding of growth, decay and changes over time.
- Shows care and concern for living things and the environment.

# ♫ *Expressive arts and design*

## *Exploring and using media and materials*

## 8–20 months

- Imitates and improvises actions they have observed, e.g. clapping or waving.
- Begins to move to music, listen to or join in rhymes or songs.
- Notices and is interested in the effects of making movements which leave marks.
- Explores and experiments with a range of media through sensory exploration, and using whole body.
- Moves whole body to enjoyable sounds, such as music or a regular beat.

## 22–36 months

- Experiments with blocks, colours and marks.
- Creates sounds by banging, shaking, tapping or blowing.

## 30–50 months

- Enjoys joining in with dancing and ring games.
- Imitates movement in response to music.
- Beginning to be interested in and describe the texture of things.
- Beginning to move rhythmically.
- Understands that they can use lines to enclose a space, and then begins to use these shapes to represent objects.
- Uses various construction materials.

## 40–60 months

- Explores what happens when they mix colours.
- Experiments to create different textures.
- Manipulates materials to achieve a planned effect.
- Constructs with a purpose in mind, using a variety of resources.
- Uses simple tools and techniques competently and appropriately.

## *Being imaginative*

## 16–26 months

- Expresses self through physical action and sound.
- Pretends that one object represents another, especially when objects have characteristics in common.

## 22–36 months

- Beginning to make-believe by pretending.

## 30–50 months

- Creates movement in response to music.
- Makes up rhythms.
- Uses available resources to create props to support role-play.
- Captures experiences and responses with a range of media, such as music, dance and paint and other materials or words.
- Engages in imaginative role-play based on own first-hand experiences.

- Builds stories around toys, e.g. farm animals needing rescue from an armchair 'cliff'.
- Uses available resources to create props to support role-play.

## 40–60 months

- Chooses particular colours to use for a purpose.
- Plays alongside other children who are engaged in the same theme.
- Introduces a storyline or narrative into their play.
- Creates simple representations of events, people and objects.

Development Matters in the Early Years Foundation Stage (EYFS): © Crown copyright 2012.

# 4 | April

It's important to fire the imagination, and help children develop a deeper understanding by 'making things real'. When we tell a story, whether it's to an individual or a group, we are building a common landscape together. We create the picture that's in our mind with the words we choose, and then we hopefully transfer it to the minds of our audience. To enhance the experience we can use props, or settings, which complement our words. We get them involved so that they can take ownership of the landscape and become immersed in the pictures we have created. With this in mind, the activities this month are about building a common landscape, using words, pictures and our surroundings as stepping stones to learning.

## Ridván – sunset 21st April to sunset on 2nd May

One of the most important Bahai festivals, this celebrates the time that the prophet Baha'u'llah spent in the garden of Ridvár in 1863. It's also the time when he announced that he was the prophet promised by the Bab. The key holy dates are the 1st, the 9th and the 12th, as these commemorate his arrival and departure from the garden. On these dates, prayers are said and no work is carried out. Celebrations centre around the garden. The word Ridván means paradise, and this sacred space was thought to be of exceptional beauty. Today followers celebrate in a number of ways. Many create their own Ridván garden, using white muslin drapes, to create a comfortable space outside where they can pray and give thanks.

## Garden of paradise

Turn the classroom into a garden of paradise. Explain that you're going to create a magical space, where you can tell stories, recite poems and have lots of fun. Start by asking the group to think about the colours they might use and why. Go through each colour and think about words to describe it. Use curtains, drapes, mats and cushions to create a comfortable haven, and ask the children to get involved positioning things. Once you have a space set up, gather the children around for some storytelling. If you have a favourite picture book, you can use it, or make up your own 'paradise' tale about a magical garden. So you might say:

> Billy stood before a golden door. He knew that if he opened the door, it would lead him to a magical place, a beautiful garden called Paradise. He took a deep breath and opened the door. As he walked through he could see . . . and . . . and . . . He could also smell . . . and . . . and . . . He looked around and he could hear . . . and . . . and . . . He reached out and he could touch . . . and . . . and . . .

Encourage the children to fill in the blanks. Get them to use all their senses to make this magical garden real. Once you have built up a picture of the garden, split the children into groups and get them involved in making some of the things that Billy encounters. For example, you might have one group creating colourful flowers with tissue paper, and another group drawing trees that you can stick on the wall. When they've completed this task, you can arrange the items they've created in your Ridván garden and use it as a special storytelling space.

# St George's Day – April 23rd

The patron saint of England, St George is a mystery in many ways. He appears as a mythical character associated with bravery and honour. Although he is the patron saint of England, he was actually born in Turkey and became a Roman soldier. George has a long list of accolades and is also known as the saint of soldiers, archers, cavalry, farmers and field workers. His deeds appear in myth and legend and he is closely linked to chivalry. Some even believe he had the power to help those suffering with the plague! One of the most famous tales tells how George defeated the dragon with his spear and saved the King's daughter from death.

## Dragon's den

This is a great opportunity for some imaginative storytelling. Start by telling the basic tale of how George defeated the dragon. If you have hand puppets, you can demonstrate this, or use pictures and actions to create the atmosphere. Get the children to join in, and take turns playing George and the dragon. Encourage them to think about how the dragon would move, and the kinds of noises it would make. This is something you can do together, by getting the entire group to pretend they are dragons, and to move in a circle, using their arms as wings, and making dragon noises.

Next think about George. If he was a great warrior, he might carry a spear and a sword. How might he use them? Put a sequence of actions together, and again in a group run through them. To follow on from this, ask the group to create their own dragon; they can do this individually by drawing pictures. Start with basics: how big is he, can he fly, does he breathe fire, what colour is he? With older children you can be more creative – get them to think of any special powers that their dragon might have. For example, can he talk, read minds, or turn invisible? Ask them where he might live and get them to draw a picture. Fire the imagination and give some examples, like a cave, a castle, at the bottom of a well, under the bed. Get them to put as much detail as they can in the pictures they draw, and help them make connections, by asking questions about the dragon and what he does. From this a story will develop that they can share with the rest of the group.

### Top tip

Make this a storytelling game, by using picture cards that the children have made. Start by asking the children to draw different types of dragon on the same-sized card. Then ask them to draw the dragon's den, and finally what kind of power the dragon has. Mix the cards up and place them in the centre of the room. Split the children into smaller groups and get them to pick three or four cards. From this they have to make a story about their dragon. Depending on age, they can do this by drawing pictures, writing and narrating, or acting the story out. Younger children can contribute with sound and movement to enhance the tale. The story doesn't have to be complicated. For example, it can be a simple day in the life of the dragon. Encourage the groups to think about whether their dragon is good or evil. Perhaps he doesn't like scaring people and he's a friendly dragon who helps others. Give them lots of options and let them explore and come up with their own ideas.

Create a dragon's den for them to use as a stage for their performance. Encourage them to help by draping material over tables and chairs, to create a cave-like structure. The key is to spark their imagination, so this doesn't have to be perfect. You are using props to help them picture the story.

### Create a creature

Dragons are mythical beasts and they come in all shapes and sizes. Encourage the group to create a new creature with superpowers, using the dragon as a starting point. So you might say, 'The dragon has wings in this picture. Do we want our new creature to have wings?' Then together you can count how many wings. Think about other things that dragons have and if you might want to include them. Take other animals and compare them to your creation. For example, your mythical beast might have a cat's head and an elephant's body. Give the children a range of pictures of different types of animal and explain that they can use body parts from each to create something new and magical. Finally ask them to think about how their creature moves and what kind of noises it makes. Do this by comparing it with other animals. So you might say, 'A snake wriggles and hisses' and encourage the children to join in, and then you might ask, 'Does your creature wriggle and hiss like the snake?'

### Top tip

With younger children use the mythical form of the dragon to introduce them to colour and shape. Create dragon cards using the same outline of the dragon, but with each one shaded in a different colour. Hold them up in front of the group, and ask the children to guess the colour. Give the outlines out and ask the children to colour in their dragon using three different shades. Get them to think about the shape of the dragon by tracing their fingers over the outline and describing it.

## Vaisakhi – 13th or 14th April

This Sikh new year festival usually falls on the 13th or 14th of April. The celebration also marks the year 1699 when Sikhism was born as a faith. Vaisakhi is believed to be a harvest festival and is celebrated with dancing, singing and parades throughout the day. Farmers give thanks for their crops and pray for future prosperity. It's a colourful event and many Sikhs choose to be baptised into the brotherhood on this day. The Hindus believe that thousands of years ago the goddess Ganga descended to earth, and so many Sikhs spend the day bathing in the Ganges as a form of worship.

## Washing ritual

Incorporate a washing ritual into playtime, by using bowls of warm water to represent the river Ganges. Start by encouraging the children to dip their fingers into the water and wiggle them about. Encourage them to have fun with the water, splashing and making ripples and waves like the sea. Think about shapes in the water and get them to use their hands and fingers to create different kinds of waves and bubbles. Use toy boats and objects that float and get them to imagine that they are sailing down the river. Talk about the feel of the water, and use words to describe it. Finally come up with a watery chant using words and actions combined from the previous activities. So, something like, 'I splash about in the water, I clap my hands together. I swish and splosh and slosh and splish, I make a very watery wish!' Repeat this and add more words and actions.

### Top tip

Take your chant on the move, so give it some actions, and get the children to come together and form the sea across the room. Think about how the sea moves, how it twists and turns, and get the children to sway and move together creating waves. Think about the sea on a beautiful sunny day, and the difference between this and a stormy day. Change the mood of the sea by using music to demonstrate what it is like when it's calm, and then what it's like when it's windy.

## Farmyard fun

As Vaisakhi is a harvest festival and a time for farmers to express their gratitude, create your own farmyard scene using pictures and props and asking the children to take on different roles. Start by splitting them into groups. Each group is going to play a part; for example, one group might represent

the crops growing in the earth, the other, the farmyard animals, and you might have one group to represent the farmer and his workers. Ask each group to think about their role. So the crops might consider where they would grow, how they would grow and what they might be used for. The animals might think about who they are – cows, pigs, geese – and where they might live on the farm. The farmer and his workers might think about the kinds of everyday activities that they have to do on the farm. Finally, make a map of the room and designate areas, so you might have the farmhouse where the farmer lives, the field where the crops grow, the stalls and stables where the animals live. Each group should take control of their area, and try and recreate it. Encourage them to think of simple words and phrases to describe what their role is, then take it in turns to move around the room and talk about the farm and what each area is used for.

## Top tip

With older children you can encourage them to write a story from the perspective of the character they play. For example, what's it like to be a crop growing in a farmer's field? Encourage them to describe what it's like living beneath the earth. They can then describe how it feels to break through the soil and see the sun for the first time. Get creative and ask them to choose anything related to the harvest, and give it a voice. They can write a poem or a song, or draw pictures to tell the tale.

## Development matters covered

Below you will find a list of key development matters covered in the activities above.

## Personal, social and emotional development

### Making relationships

22–36 months

* Interested in others' play and starting to join in.
* Seeks out others to share experiences.

30–50 months

* Can play in a group, extending and elaborating play ideas, e.g. building up a role-play activity with other children.
* Initiates play, offering cues to peers to join them.
* Keeps play going by responding to what others are saying or doing.

- Demonstrates friendly behaviour, initiating conversations and forming good relationships with peers and familiar adults.

## Self-confidence and self-awareness

### 16–26 months

- Explores new toys and environments, but 'checks in' regularly with familiar adult as and when needed.
- Gradually able to engage in pretend play with toys (supports child to understand their own thinking may be different from others').

### 30–50 months

- Can select and use activities and resources with help.

# Communication and language

## Listening and attention

### 8–20 months

- Has a strong exploratory impulse.
- Concentrates intently on an object or activity of own choosing for short periods.

### 16–26 months

- Listens to and enjoys rhythmic patterns in rhymes and stories.
- Enjoys rhymes and demonstrates listening by trying to join in with actions or vocalisation.

### 22–36 months

- Listens with interest to the noises adults make when they read stories.
- Shows interest in play with sounds, songs and rhymes.

### 30–50 months

- Listens to others one to one or in small groups, when conversation interests them.
- Joins in with repeated refrains and anticipates key events and phrases in rhymes and stories.

- Is able to follow directions (if not intently focused on own choice of activity).
- Listens to stories with increasing attention and recall.

## Understanding

### 16–26 months

- Understands simple sentences, e.g. 'Throw the ball.'

### 22–36 months

- Understands more complex sentences, e.g. 'Put your toys away and then we'll read a book.'
- Understands 'who', 'what', 'where' in simple questions, e.g. Who's that/who can? What's that? Where is . . .?

### 30–50 months

- Understands use of objects, e.g. 'What do we use to cut things?'
- Responds to simple instructions, e.g. to get or put away an object.
- Beginning to understand 'why' and 'how' questions.

### 40–60 months

- Able to follow a story without pictures or props.
- Listens and responds to ideas expressed by others in conversation or discussion.

## Speaking

### 8–20 months

- Frequently imitates words and sounds.
- Enjoys babbling and increasingly experiments with using sounds and words to communicate for a range of purposes, e.g. teddy, more, no, bye-bye.
- Uses sounds in play, e.g. 'brrrm' for toy car.
- Uses single words.

### 16–26 months

- Uses different types of everyday words (nouns, verbs and adjectives, e.g. banana, go, sleep, hot).
- Beginning to ask simple questions.

## 22–36 months

- Learns new words very rapidly and is able to use them in communicating.
- Uses gestures, sometimes with limited talk, e.g. reaches toward toy, saying 'I have it'.
- Uses a variety of questions, e.g. what, where, who.
- Uses simple sentences, e.g. 'Mummy gonna work.'
- Uses language as a powerful means of widening contacts, sharing feelings, experiences and thoughts.
- Holds a conversation, jumping from topic to topic.

## 30–50 months

- Beginning to use more complex sentences to link thoughts, e.g. using 'and' and 'because'.
- Uses talk to connect ideas, explain what is happening and anticipate what might happen next, recall and relive past experiences.
- Questions why things happen and gives explanations. Asks e.g. who, what, when, how.
- Builds up vocabulary that reflects the breadth of their experiences.
- Uses talk in pretending that objects stand for something else in play, e,g, 'This box is my castle.'

## 40–60 months

- Uses language to imagine and recreate roles and experiences in play situations.
- Introduces a storyline or narrative into their play.
- Extends vocabulary, especially by grouping and naming, exploring the meaning and sounds of new words.

## *Physical development*

### *Moving and handling*

## 8–20 months

- Crawls, bottom shuffles or rolls continuously to move around.
- Picks up small objects between thumb and fingers.
- Enjoys the sensory experience of making marks in damp sand, paste or paint.
- Holds pen or crayon using a whole hand (palmar) grasp and makes random marks with different strokes.

## 22–36 months

- Shows control in holding and using jugs to pour, hammers, books and mark-making tools.
- Squats with steadiness to rest or play with object on the ground, and rises to feet without using hands.
- Beginning to use three fingers (tripod grip) to hold writing tools.
- Imitates drawing simple shapes such as circles and lines.

## 30–50 months

- Draws lines and circles using gross motor movements.
- Uses one-handed tools and equipment, e.g. makes snips in paper with child scissors.
- Moves freely and with pleasure and confidence in a range of ways, such as slithering, shuffling, rolling, crawling, walking, running, jumping, skipping, sliding and hopping.

## 40–60 months

- Uses simple tools to effect changes to materials.
- Handles tools, objects, construction and malleable materials safely and with increasing control.
- Experiments with different ways of moving.

### *Health and self-care*

## 30–50 months

- Can usually manage washing and drying hands.

# Literacy

### *Reading*

## 22–36 months

- Has some favourite stories, rhymes, songs, poems or jingles.
- Repeats words or phrases from familiar stories.

## 30–50 months

- Enjoys rhyming and rhythmic activities.
- Shows awareness of rhyme and alliteration.
- Listens to and joins in with stories and poems, one to one and also in small groups.
- Joins in with repeated refrains and anticipates key events and phrases in rhymes and stories.
- Beginning to be aware of the way stories are structured.
- Suggests how the story might end.
- Listens to stories with increasing attention and recall.
- Describes main story settings, events and principal characters.
- Shows interest in illustrations and print in books and print in the environment.

## 40–60 months

- Uses vocabulary and forms of speech that are increasingly influenced by their experiences of books.
- Continues a rhyming string.
- Hears and says the initial sound in words.

### *Writing*

## 30–50 months

- Sometimes gives meaning to marks as they draw and paint.

## 40–60 months

- Gives meaning to marks they make as they draw, write and paint.
- Begins to break the flow of speech into words.
- Continues a rhyming string.

# *Mathematics*

### *Shape, space and measure*

## 16–26 months

- Uses blocks to create their own simple structures and arrangements.
- Enjoys filling and emptying containers.

## 22–36 months

- Notices simple shapes and patterns in pictures.

## 30–50 months

- Shows an interest in shape and space by playing with shapes or making arrangements with objects.
- Shows interest in shapes in the environment.
- Uses shapes appropriately for tasks.
- Beginning to talk about the shapes of everyday objects, e.g. 'round' and 'tall'.

## 40–60 months

- Uses familiar objects and common shapes to create and recreate patterns and build models.

# Understanding the world

## The world

## 8–20 months

- Becomes absorbed in combining objects, e.g. banging two objects or placing objects into containers.

## 16–26 months

- Explores objects by linking together different approaches: shaking, hitting, looking, feeling, tasting, mouthing, pulling, turning and poking.
- Remembers where objects belong.
- Matches parts of objects that fit together, e.g. puts lid on teapot.

## 22–36 months

- Notices detailed features of objects in their environment.

## 30–50 months

- Comments and asks questions about aspects of their familiar world such as the place where they live or the natural world.
- Can talk about some of the things they have observed such as plants, animals, natural and found objects.

# Expressive arts and design

## Exploring and using media and materials

### 8–20 months

- Imitates and improvises actions they have observed, e.g. clapping or waving.
- Begins to move to music, listen to or join in rhymes or songs.
- Notices and is interested in the effects of making movements which leave marks.
- Explores and experiments with a range of media through sensory exploration, and using whole body.
- Moves whole body to enjoyable sounds, such as music or a regular beat.

### 22–36 months

- Experiments with blocks, colours and marks.
- Creates sounds by banging, shaking, tapping or blowing.

### 30–50 months

- Enjoys joining in with dancing and ring games.
- Imitates movement in response to music.
- Beginning to be interested in and describe the texture of things.
- Beginning to move rhythmically.
- Understands that they can use lines to enclose a space, and then begin to use these shapes to represent objects.
- Uses various construction materials.
- Beginning to construct, stacking blocks vertically and horizontally, making enclosures and creating spaces.
- Joins construction pieces together to build and balance.
- Realises tools can be used for a purpose.

### 40–60 months

- Explores what happens when they mix colours.
- Experiments to create different textures.
- Manipulates materials to achieve a planned effect.
- Constructs with a purpose in mind, using a variety of resources.
- Uses simple tools and techniques competently and appropriately.
- Selects tools and techniques needed to shape, assemble and join materials they are using.

## Being imaginative

### 16–26 months

- Expresses self through physical action and sound.
- Pretends that one object represents another, especially when objects have characteristics in common.

### 22–36 months

- Beginning to make-believe by pretending.

### 30–50 months

- Creates movement in response to music.
- Makes up rhythms.
- Uses available resources to create props to support role-play.
- Captures experiences and responses with a range of media, such as music, dance and paint and other materials or words.
- Engages in imaginative role-play based on own first-hand experiences.
- Builds stories around toys, e.g. farm animals needing rescue from an armchair 'cliff'.
- Uses available resources to create props to support role-play.

### 40–60 months

- Chooses particular colours to use for a purpose.
- Plays alongside other children who are engaged in the same theme.
- Plays cooperatively as part of a group to develop and act out a narrative.
- Introduces a storyline or narrative into their play.
- Creates simple representations of events, people and objects.

Development Matters in the Early Years Foundation Stage (EYFS): © Crown copyright 2012.

# 5 | May

May is in an interesting month. Spring has finally sprung, and there's a feeling of growth and new life in the air which extends to some of the festivals that we celebrate. Change is all around us, and the landscape reflects this with colour and movement. Use this as an opportunity to be more aware of the environment; take note of the little things that make up the bigger picture. Look up to the sky for inspiration and match creative activities and games to these celebrations from around the world.

## Beltane fun

May 1st or May Day, as it's now referred to, marks the beginning of the ancient festival of Beltane, named after the Celtic fire god Bel. This festival celebrates the light and moving into the spring and summer. The people would light fires to welcome the sun into their life. They believed the sun had life-giving and cleansing properties and that, through fire, they could cleanse themselves and the land in preparation for a good harvest. The Triple Goddess worshipped by the ancients was in her maiden phase at this time, so she was thought of as the Spring Bride or May Queen. Young maidens followed suit as part of the celebrations and dressed up in pretty dresses adorned with flowers, to represent fertility and new growth. Men and women would join hands and make a circle around the fire, whilst singing and dancing to welcome the light into their life.

## Mr Sun

To make this activity fun and help the children engage with the idea that the sun is an entity, you are going to turn it into a character. Encourage the children to help with this by asking questions. What would the sun look like? Would he/she be a boy or a girl? Would he/she have arms and legs? What else would he/she need – eyes, ears? Where would he/she live? What would he/she do every day?

Split the children into smaller groups and get them to draw a picture of Mr or Mrs Sun. Encourage them to describe their character verbally and talk about a typical day in the life of the sun. What does he or she get up to? Think about how the sun moves through the sky, and encourage little ones to move around the room, and pretend they are the sun. What kind of action or sound illustrates the sun getting brighter?

With older children, you might ask them to think how the sun's movements vary through the sky. Does it appear to speed up or slow down at particular times of the day? Why does this happen? Maybe the sun gets tired, or has more energy in the morning. Have fun with this, and encourage them to make up stories about the sun's adventures.

### Top tip

Think about other cultures and their interpretation of the sun. Many have their own set of tales to explain its movements. For example, the Egyptians believed that the sun god, Ra, would carry the sun on his chariot through the sky during the day. At night he would disappear to fight the demon serpent Apep, only to reappear in the morning and begin his journey again. Imagine if you could carry the sun through the sky. What would you carry it on – a bus, a fire engine, maybe a train? With older groups of children take this opportunity to create your own sun chariot, using chairs, and paper and any other decoration you have to hand. Encourage them to take turns sitting on the chariot, firing it up for the day. Get them to use sounds and actions as it travels through the sky.

Give the groups the opportunity to share their pictures and tales with the rest of the class, and if you've created a sun chariot, use it as centre stage for their presentation.

## Sun circle

Have your own Beltane celebration by combining the idea of the sun and the circle, an important shape in Celtic mythology. Start by getting the group into a large circle. Now make a pretend sun that you can place in the centre of a circle, by drawing a large golden orb. Get the group to help you colour it in, taking smaller sections of the sun that you can all work on. Next tell a simple tale about the sun to the group. Explain that as the sun is born each morning, it rises in the sky to look down upon us. Then talk about its power, how it shines and brings light and warmth. With older children you can talk about why this is important. What other creatures might need the sun's light and heat to survive?

Create a chant by listing descriptive words associated with the sun, and repeating them. So you might say, 'Sun shines bright, sun shines light,' and at the same time think of actions to go with this, so you might stretch out your arms to represent the sun, and wiggle your fingers to represent it shining and casting light and warmth upon the earth. Encourage little ones to do the same. Hold hands and move around the circle, going from one direction to another. Say, 'I move round and round the circle, I spin like the sun. Round and round the circle until the day is done!' Finish by dancing around the circle and repeating your chant.

## Top tip

With older children, talk about the May Queen. Encourage them to think about how she would dress. What would she wear? What colour flowers would she carry or wear? What else might she have to show that she's a queen? Have a go at some role play and get them to dress up as the May Queen. Encourage them to use bits of material and tissue paper to represent the colourful flowers and to make any other props. Finish with a procession to herald the coming of the May Queen and play some music to encourage movement and dance.

## Parent fun

Hold a family event to mark May Day and include some of the activities above, like the sun circle and the May Queen procession. Set up tables and stalls and include lots of springtime treats and games.

## Visakha Puja Day or Buddha Day

Thought to be the holiest of all Buddhist holidays, this festival is celebrated during the full moon of May every year. Commonly known as Buddha Day, it's believed to be the day that Buddha was born. It also coincides with the day he died and passed on to the state of Nirvana. On this day most temples leave offerings of food, and celebrate the goodness of Buddha. In the evening they hold candlelit processions through the streets.

### Full-moon dance

Since we focused on the sun for our Beltane activities, it seems fitting to look at the power of the moon to celebrate Buddha Day. Start by describing how the moon moves through the sky, how it changes every night and appears to grow bigger, until it reaches its full-moon phase, and then how it starts to grow smaller until it seems to disappear from the sky. Encourage the children to be like the moon, starting off very small and curled up, and then slowly getting bigger, stretching out, until they can stand and become the full moon. Repeat these movements to music, and go back and forth from full moon to waning moon. Explain that even when they're at their smallest curled-up stage, they're still there. Just like the moon – we think we cannot see it but it's still there shining in the sky. Finish this activity by getting the children to sit like Buddha, to close their eyes and listen. Ask them what kind of animals might come out beneath the moon and encourage them to make animal sounds and movements.

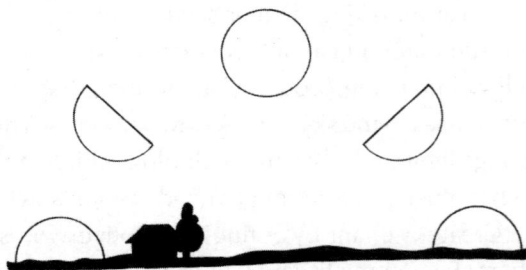

### Top tip

Encourage the children to come up with words associated with the moon, and if possible put them in a rhyme. Get them to think about the appearance of the moon. Does it remind them of anything – a giant piece of cheese, a snowball? How would they describe it? With older children you can take the opportunity to point out the differences between the sun and the moon. This should be obvious in the choice of words to describe them.

## Lag B'omer

This minor Jewish festival occurs on the 33rd day of the Counting of Omer, which is a time of mourning; however, the festival itself is a celebration, and marks a day of parties, marriages and special events. There are different beliefs about the origins of Lag B'omer and why it is celebrated. Some believe it marks the end of a terrible plague; others that it represents one day in history, when the Jews won a victory over Rome. Traditionally, bonfires are lit throughout Israel, and children are taken to the park to play with bows and arrows. The bow is important as it relates to the fact that a rainbow never appeared in the sky during Rabbi Shimon's lifetime and this was seen as a good omen.

## Rainbow magic

Although it was considered bad luck to see a rainbow, many traditions around the world think differently. Whatever your point of view, rainbows are fabulous visual tools that children can enjoy. Start by showing the children a giant picture of a rainbow and then help them to draw their own version. What colours might they include and why? Encourage them to think about the size and shape of the rainbow. As they colour in each shade ask them to think of other things that are the same colour or shape, and make up lists as you go along.

With older children you can turn this into a storytelling exercise. Start by telling them the story of a magic rainbow. Make it simple. Something along the lines of, 'One day a magic rainbow appeared in the sky. Billy and Sally thought it looked very pretty and decided to follow it. They walked and skipped and ran, until they reached the end. And that's when they saw a . . .'

Ask them to draw what Billy and Sally found at the end of the rainbow. Give them some ideas, and then split into smaller groups to come up with pictures and stories. Have fun with this, and use other picture books to come up with ideas. When you've finished give everyone the chance to show their picture.

## Further activities

If you decide to use all three festivals, then make them work for you and create a sky collage that you can display on the wall. Incorporate drawings of the sun, the moon and also include a giant rainbow and anything else that you might see in the sky. At this point encourage the children to use their imagination. What else flies? For example they might want to draw in a balloon, some birds, an aeroplane, or even a fairy. The sky is the limit!

Use key words, rhymes and chants that you have created together that describe the movement of planets through the sky. You can incorporate these into your collage, matching words with objects.

**Top tip**

Turn this activity on its head, and create a similar scene, but this time as a giant floor mat. Or split the scene into separate drawings of the sun, moon, a rainbow and various other flying objects and place them in different spots upon the floor. Get the children moving around the room. Ask them to imagine that they have wings and they're flying through the sky. Play some music, then when it stops, they have to choose a picture to sit on. Play this game so that everyone has the chance to pick a different picture.

# Pentecost or Whitsun

This festival celebrates the birth of the Christian Church. It falls on a Sunday, 50 days after Easter, and is used to worship the presence of the Holy Spirit. In Church, ministers will often wear red robes to represent the flame of the Holy Spirit. The wind is often associated with this festival, because it was thought that the apostles were celebrating the harvest festival when the Holy Spirit came down. It was like a powerful wind, and literally took their breath away, causing them to speak in what sounded like a foreign language.

## Windy weather

Start by thinking about the wind. What does it sound like? Get the group to make some noise, starting first with a gentle 'whoosh' for the breeze and increasing in volume as the wind gets more powerful. So they might want to stamp their feet or wave some card or paper to make rumbling sounds. Think about words that describe the wind and string them together. So you might say, 'The wind is blowing at my door, it's whooshing, shooshing, whooing, whirring . . .' and encourage younger children to make the noises with you.

If the wind was a character, what would he/she look like? He/she might be shaped like a cloud, or a round blob. Encourage the children to have a go at drawing the wind, and to think about the colours and shapes they would use. How does the wind feel? Is he/she angry or sad? Perhaps he/she is excited and the stronger he/she gets, the happier he/she is.

With older children, get them thinking about the power of the wind. Is it more powerful than the sun because it can blow things over? Tell them the fable of the wind and the sun, how they were arguing one day over which one was stronger. On seeing a traveller coming down the road they set each other a challenge. Whoever could get the traveller to remove his cloak would be the strongest. The wind blew with all his might, but the traveller held on to his cloak tightly. When it was the sun's turn he beamed down upon the traveller in all his glory, making him so hot, he had to remove his cloak. Ask the children to help you act this out.

# Development matters covered

Below you will find a list of key development matters covered in the activities above.

## *Personal, social and emotional development*

### *Making relationships*

### 22–36 months

- Interested in others' play and starting to join in.
- Seeks out others to share experiences.

### 30–50 months

- Can play in a group, extending and elaborating play ideas, e.g. building up a role-play activity with other children.
- Initiates play, offering cues to peers to join them.
- Keeps play going by responding to what others are saying or doing.
- Demonstrates friendly behaviour, initiating conversations and forming good relationships with peers and familiar adults.

### *Self-confidence and self-awareness*

### 16–26 months

- Explores new toys and environments, but 'checks in' regularly with familiar adult as and when needed.

- Gradually able to engage in pretend play with toys (supports child to understand their own thinking may be different from others').

## 30–50 months

- Can select and use activities and resources with help.

# 💬 *Communication and language*

## *Listening and attention*

### 8–20 months

- Has a strong exploratory impulse.
- Concentrates intently on an object or activity of own choosing for short periods.

### 16–26 months

- Listens to and enjoys rhythmic patterns in rhymes and stories.
- Enjoys rhymes and demonstrates listening by trying to join in with actions or vocalisation.

### 22–36 months

- Listens with interest to the noises adults make when they read stories.
- Shows interest in play with sounds, songs and rhymes.

### 30–50 months

- Listens to others one to one or in small groups, when conversation interests them.
- Joins in with repeated refrains and anticipates key events and phrases in rhymes and stories.
- Is able to follow directions (if not intently focused on own choice of activity).
- Listens to stories with increasing attention and recall.

## *Understanding*

### 16–26 months

- Understands simple sentences, e.g. 'Throw the ball.'

## 22–36 months

- Understands more complex sentences, e.g. 'Put your toys away and then we'll read a book.'
- Understands 'who', 'what', 'where' in simple questions, e.g. Who's that/who can? What's that? Where is . . .?

## 30–50 months

- Understands use of objects, e.g. 'What do we use to cut things?'
- Responds to simple instructions, e.g. to get or put away an object.
- Beginning to understand 'why' and 'how' questions.

## 40–60 months

- Able to follow a story without pictures or props.
- Listens and responds to ideas expressed by others in conversation or discussion.

### *Speaking*

## 8–20 months

- Frequently imitates words and sounds.
- Enjoys babbling and increasingly experiments with using sounds and words to communicate for a range of purposes, e.g. teddy, more, no, bye-bye.
- Uses sounds in play, e.g. 'brrrm' for toy car.
- Uses single words.

## 16–26 months

- Uses different types of everyday words (nouns, verbs and adjectives, e.g. banana, go, sleep, hot).
- Beginning to ask simple questions.

## 22–36 months

- Learns new words very rapidly and is able to use them in communicating.
- Uses gestures, sometimes with limited talk, e.g. reaches toward toy, saying 'I have it'.
- Uses a variety of questions, e.g. what, where, who.
- Uses simple sentences, e.g. 'Mummy gonna work.'

- Uses language as a powerful means of widening contacts, sharing feelings, experiences and thoughts.
- Holds a conversation, jumping from topic to topic.

## 30–50 months

- Beginning to use more complex sentences to link thoughts, e.g. using 'and' and 'because').
- Uses talk to connect ideas, explain what is happening and anticipate what might happen next, recall and relive past experiences.
- Questions why things happen and gives explanations. Asks e.g. who, what, when, how.
- Builds up vocabulary that reflects the breadth of their experiences.
- Uses talk in pretending that objects stand for something else in play, e.g. 'This box is my castle.'

## 40–60 months

- Uses language to imagine and recreate roles and experiences in play situations.
- Introduces a storyline or narrative into their play.
- Extends vocabulary, especially by grouping and naming, exploring the meaning and sounds of new words.

## *Physical development*

### *Moving and handling*

### 8–20 months

- Crawls, bottom shuffles or rolls continuously to move around.
- Picks up small objects between thumb and fingers.
- Enjoys the sensory experience of making marks in damp sand, paste or paint.
- Holds pen or crayon using a whole hand (palmar) grasp and makes random marks with different strokes.

### 22–36 months

- Shows control in holding and using jugs to pour, hammers, books and mark-making tools.
- Squats with steadiness to rest or play with object on the ground, and rises to feet without using hands.

- Beginning to use three fingers (tripod grip) to hold writing tools.
- Imitates drawing simple shapes such as circles and lines.

## 30–50 months

- Draws lines and circles using gross motor movements.
- Uses one-handed tools and equipment, e.g. makes snips in paper with child scissors.
- Moves freely and with pleasure and confidence in a range of ways, such as slithering, shuffling, rolling, crawling, walking, running, jumping, skipping, sliding and hopping.

## 40–60 months

- Uses simple tools to effect changes to materials.
- Handles tools, objects, construction and malleable materials safely and with increasing control.
- Experiments with different ways of moving.

### Health and self-care

## 30–50 months

- Can usually manage washing and drying hands.

# Literacy

### Reading

## 22–36 months

- Has some favourite stories, rhymes, songs, poems or jingles.
- Repeats words or phrases from familiar stories.

## 30–50 months

- Enjoys rhyming and rhythmic activities.
- Shows awareness of rhyme and alliteration.
- Listens to and joins in with stories and poems, one to one and also in small groups.

- Joins in with repeated refrains and anticipates key events and phrases in rhymes and stories.
- Beginning to be aware of the way stories are structured.
- Suggests how the story might end.
- Listens to stories with increasing attention and recall.
- Describes main story settings, events and principal characters.
- Shows interest in illustrations and print in books and print in the environment.

## 40–60 months

- Uses vocabulary and forms of speech that are increasingly influenced by their experiences of books.
- Continues a rhyming string.
- Hears and says the initial sound in words.

### Writing

## 30–50 months

- Sometimes gives meaning to marks as they draw and paint.

## 40–60 months

- Gives meaning to marks they make as they draw, write and paint.
- Begins to break the flow of speech into words.
- Continues a rhyming string.

# Mathematics

### Shape, space and measure

## 16–26 months

- Uses blocks to create their own simple structures and arrangements.
- Enjoys filling and emptying containers.

## 22–36 months

- Notices simple shapes and patterns in pictures.

## 30–50 months

- Shows an interest in shape and space by playing with shapes or making arrangements with objects.
- Shows interest in shapes in the environment.
- Uses shapes appropriately for tasks.
- Beginning to talk about the shapes of everyday objects, e.g. 'round' and 'tall'.

## 40–60 months

- Uses familiar objects and common shapes to create and recreate patterns and build models.

# Understanding the world

*The world*

## 8–20 months

- Becomes absorbed in combining objects, e.g. banging two objects or placing objects into containers.

## 16–26 months

- Explores objects by linking together different approaches: shaking, hitting, looking, feeling, tasting, mouthing, pulling, turning and poking.
- Remembers where objects belong.
- Matches parts of objects that fit together, e.g. puts lid on teapot.

## 22–36 months

- Notices detailed features of objects in their environment.

## 30–50 months

- Comments and asks questions about aspects of their familiar world such as the place where they live or the natural world.
- Can talk about some of the things they have observed such as plants, animals, natural and found objects.

## 🎵 *Expressive arts and design*

### *Exploring and using media and materials*

### 8–20 months

- Imitates and improvises actions they have observed, e.g. clapping or waving.
- Begins to move to music, listen to or join in rhymes or songs.
- Notices and is interested in the effects of making movements which leave marks.
- Explores and experiments with a range of media through sensory exploration, and using whole body.
- Moves whole body to enjoyable sounds, such as music or a regular beat.

### 22–36 months

- Experiments with blocks, colours and marks.
- Creates sounds by banging, shaking, tapping or blowing.

### 30–50 months

- Enjoys joining in with dancing and ring games.
- Imitates movement in response to music.
- Beginning to be interested in and describe the texture of things.
- Beginning to move rhythmically.
- Understands that they can use lines to enclose a space, and then begin to use these shapes to represent objects.
- Uses various construction materials.
- Beginning to construct, stacking blocks vertically and horizontally, making enclosures and creating spaces.
- Joins construction pieces together to build and balance.
- Realises tools can be used for a purpose.

### 40–60 months

- Explores what happens when they mix colours.
- Experiments to create different textures.
- Manipulates materials to achieve a planned effect.
- Constructs with a purpose in mind, using a variety of resources.
- Uses simple tools and techniques competently and appropriately.

- Selects tools and techniques needed to shape, assemble and join materials they are using.

## Being imaginative

### 16–26 months

- Expresses self through physical action and sound.
- Pretends that one object represents another, especially when objects have characteristics in common.

### 22–36 months

- Beginning to make-believe by pretending.

### 30–50 months

- Creates movement in response to music.
- Makes up rhythms.
- Uses available resources to create props to support role-play.
- Captures experiences and responses with a range of media, such as music, dance and paint and other materials or words.
- Engages in imaginative ro e-play based on own first-hand experiences.
- Builds stories around toys, e.g. farm animals needing rescue from an armchair 'cliff'.
- Uses available resources to create props to support role-play.

### 40–60 months

- Chooses particular colours to use for a purpose.
- Plays alongside other children who are engaged in the same theme.
- Plays cooperatively as part of a group to develop and act out a narrative.
- Introduces a storyline or narrative into their play.
- Creates simple representations of events, people and objects.

Development Matters in the Early Years Foundation Stage (EYFS): © Crown copyright 2012.

# 6 | June

June is named after the Roman goddess Juno. This goddess played a nurturing role. She looked after hearth and home, and was often associated with fire and cooking. As a mother goddess, she is warm and caring, and represents new growth, which we see all around us at this time of year. With this in mind, the activities that I have linked to the festivals this month encourage young children to connect with each other, whether that's physically through movement, or by creating a common landscape and building stories and pictures. By engaging in different ways, we learn the importance of sharing experience to build common ground. This is a key skill that helps us celebrate the similarities and differences that make us who we are.

## Litha – the summer solstice

The longest day of the year, the summer solstice, which tends to fall around the 20th/21st of June, is an important event in the pagan calendar. For centuries druids would come together to worship at this time. Litha, as the festival is known, is a time to embrace and celebrate light overcoming the darkness. Our pagan ancestors would welcome the summer into their life by lighting fires, preparing great feasts with dancing, storytelling and jumping the broom, a tradition that involves couples holding hands and jumping over a broom to cement their love. The druids believed that at this time the Sun God was at his most powerful, and the goddess was pregnant with his child. It's a time of growth and fertility, when the land is awash with flowers blooming. Because of this, flowers were often collected and used to decorate homes. Today, Stonehenge is a popular destination for revellers, with many celebrating throughout the day and night.

## Sweep and jump

Take inspiration from our pagan ancestors and create a 'jump the broom' game that you can play in groups. Start by encouraging the children to pretend that they're holding a broom. Get them to think about how and what they would use it for. Demonstrate sweeping movements and encourage them to copy you. Come up with a song to help them develop a rhythm, so, something like, 'We sweep to the left, and we sweep to the right, we sweep in a circle, and we sweep day and night.' Repeat and have fun by speeding up the rhyme and the movements.

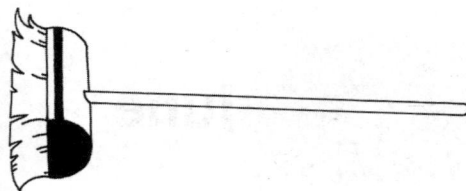

Next take the real broom (if you haven't got a broom, a brush or feather duster will do). Leave it in the centre of the room and form a circle around it. Explain that this is what our ancestors would have done, as part of the party games to celebrate the longest day. Start by holding hands and moving around the circle, going first left and then right. Increase speed, until you are skipping. Put on some music and at a suitable point stop it. The idea is that everyone must sit down as quickly as they can once the music has stopped. Those left standing must hold hands and jump over the broom together, before they can return to the circle. Repeat as often as you like, so that everyone gets a turn at jumping the broom!

### Top tip

Brooms were often used in cleansing rituals at this time, as a way of sweeping away the old. This idea often appears in folklore, and is most likely why the broom is thought of as a magical tool. Encourage older children to create their own broom. If you have access to a park or woodland area, you can gather twigs and feathers and use string to tie them together. Explain the concept of building the broom and collecting twigs of roughly the same size and shape to make it easier. Think about other natural objects that could be used. When everyone has had a go at making a broom, encourage them to move around the room, making sweeping movements. You could use your chant from the previous activities or make up a new one.

### Parent fun

Encourage the children to help around the house with cleaning activities. Introduce the idea of a good 'spring clean' and tie it in to the use of the broom in cleansing rituals. Make this fun and get the children to create 'home help' vouchers, using colourful bits of papers with pictures. These can be exchanged in return for help with cleaning and tidying.

## Flower power

Explain that, in smaller groups, little ones are going to have a go at creating a collage of a wild flower meadow. Show them pictures of different types of flowers and encourage them to describe the shape and colours. Split them into small groups and give them paper, crayons, paints, tissue paper, felt, cotton wool, glitter and card. The idea is that they're going to construct a three-dimensional picture with lots of colour and different textures. Talk about what's in the picture together, and once they've finished, return to the larger group and give them the opportunity to present their artwork and describe it.

Finally, stick all the pictures together to create a huge wild flower meadow on the floor. Use this as the base for some group storytelling. So, get everyone sitting in a circle around the meadow. Start with something simple, so you might say, 'It was a lovely, warm, sunny day and we were sitting in a meadow.' Look to the child on the right and say, 'Lisa, what can you tell me about the meadow? What colour flowers can you see?' Move around the circle giving each child the chance to describe either what they see, or what they might be doing in the meadow, for example, sitting, standing, jumping, dancing, sleeping. Encourage them to do the actions and then repeat together as a group. You can use the meadow setting for all types of reading or story games, so that whenever the collage is placed on the floor, the group understand it's time for creative play.

Another idea to get the group outside and close to nature is to find a tree, and make it the 'storytelling' tree. As a group you can sit around the tree and tell tales. The idea is that the tree listens, so you can tell it anything you want: stories, rhymes, how you think and feel, whatever words or sounds come to mind. This is a great way to get young children talking and making lots of noise. It also helps experience their environment first-hand.

## Top tip

Give older children the chance to grow some flowers. Invest in small pots or tubs of soil and packs of seeds. Or if you have some space outside, dedicate a section for flower growing. Split the children into pairs or small groups. They must take responsibility for their pot or section of soil, planting the seeds and then watering them together.

# Corpus Christi

This festival worships the body of Christ, and is celebrated by Roman Catholics and some Christians. The idea is said to have come from a Belgium nun, who had the same dream night after night which she believed was a religious experience. In the dream she saw her church beneath a full moon, with a black spot hovering. According to legend, Christ came to her in a vision to interpret this dream. He explained that the moon was the church's calendar of festivals and that the black spot represented the lack of a festival to celebrate the body of Christ. After sharing this with her local bishop, a decree was issued in the year 1246 that this festival should go ahead. The main part of the celebrations, which include a great feast, is a procession through the city.

## *Dreamscape*

Start by talking about what happens when we go to sleep. We close our eyes, and sometimes we enter a different world. We see and hear things and can go on great adventures. Explain that when we dream, it's like we are writing our own magical story. Use a springboard story, to inspire the children to come up with their own dreamscape.

Begin by getting them to imagine that they are asleep. Encourage them to close their eyes, and describe the setting, with the moon in the sky and the stars twinkling. Then say, 'As you drift off to sleep, you feel your bed lifting into the air. You feel it flying through your window, taking you on a magical journey to another land. You open your eyes, and you look around. You know you are dreaming, but where are you? What do you see?'

Then get them to draw what they see. This is something they can do individually or in groups. Encourage them to take the next step and make connections between things, so get them to think about what happens in this place, who do they meet, how do they get home? Then spend some time at the end of the session sharing pictures and ideas.

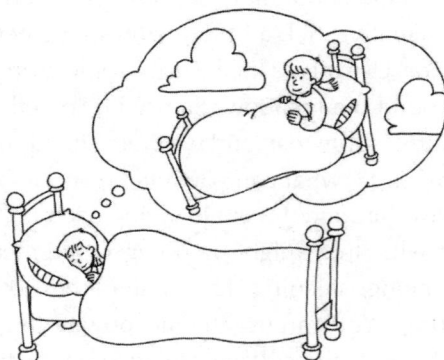

## *Top tip*

With younger children, rather than trying to come up with story ideas, think in terms of shapes and colours. Start with a song or rhyme, something like, 'When I close my eyes, what colours do I see?' and use actions to go with it, by placing hands over eyes and then opening arms wide. Use hand prints and paint in a range of different colours and get the children to make colourful scenes and patterns.

## *Procession fun*

Take the idea of the procession used by the Roman Catholics to celebrate Corpus Christi, and get the group to come up with their own 'summer' themed version. Explain that processions often occur during festivals and are a way of celebrating an event. Talk about what a procession is, for example, how do people walk, do they march together, do they play instruments and dress up? Then explain that you're going to have your own procession. Encourage the group to think about how they might move, what sounds they would make and what they would wear. Have a go at making some noise together, using different parts of the body, such as clapping, stamping, cheering. Think about what they might wear. Perhaps they'd wear bright colours to celebrate the summer or carry pictures. They could wear or carry flowers, or even dress up as a flower in bloom. Dip into your dressing-up box, and use all the materials you have to hand to help the children get into the spirit of this event.

### Top tip

Encourage older children to think about what summer means to them, and to share their thoughts and opinions. Then talk about how they might want to include their ideas in the procession. Plan a route through the classroom, taking the children on a journey outside to enjoy the sun. Make sure they take it in turns being in the lead, and get them to think about the shapes they are creating, such as circles, twisting snakes, a long straight line. Encourage them to make some noise as they go. So they might want to sing, clap, wave their hands, or shake bells. Have fun with this, and try and capture the essence of summer as you go!

# Development matters covered

Below you will find a list of key development matters covered in the activities above.

## *Personal, social and emotional development*

### Making relationships

### 8–20 months

- Interacts with others and explores new situations when supported by familiar person.
- Shows interest in the activities of others and responds differently to children and adults, e.g. may be more interested in watching children than adults or may pay more attention when children talk to them.

## 16–26 months

- Plays alongside others.
- Plays cooperatively with a familiar adult, e.g. rolling a ball back and forth.

## 30–50 months

- Can play in a group, extending and elaborating play ideas, e.g. building up a role-play activity with other children.
- Initiates play, offering cues to peers to join them.
- Keeps play going by responding to what others are saying or doing.

# 💬 *Communication and language*

## *Listening and attention*

## 8–20 months

- Has a strong exploratory impulse.
- Concentrates intently on an object or activity of own choosing for short periods.

## 16–26 months

- Listens to and enjoys rhythmic patterns in rhymes and stories.
- Enjoys rhymes and demonstrates listening by trying to join in with actions or vocalisation.

## 22–36 months

- Listens with interest to the noises adults make when they read stories.
- Shows interest in play with sounds, songs and rhymes.

## 30–50 months

- Listens to others one to one or in small groups, when conversation interests them.
- Joins in with repeated refrains and anticipates key events and phrases in rhymes and stories.

## *Understanding*

## 16–26 months

- Understands simple sentences, e.g. 'Throw the ball.'

## 30–50 months

- Understands use of objects, e.g. 'What do we use to cut things?'
- Responds to simple instructions, e.g. to get or put away an object.

## 40–60 months

- Able to follow a story without pictures or props.
- Listens and responds to ideas expressed by others in conversation or discussion.

# Physical development

## Moving and handling

### 8–20 months

- Pulls to standing, holding on to furniture or person for support.
- Crawls, bottom shuffles or rolls continuously to move around.
- Walks around furniture lifting one foot and stepping sideways (cruising), and walks with one or both hands held by adult.
- Picks up small objects between thumb and fingers.
- Enjoys the sensory experience of making marks in damp sand, paste or paint.
- Holds pen or crayon using a whole hand (palmar) grasp and makes random marks with different strokes.

### 22–36 months

- Shows control in holding and using jugs to pour, hammers, books and mark-making tools.
- Beginning to use three fingers (tripod grip) to hold writing tools.
- Imitates drawing simple shapes such as circles and lines.

### 30–50 months

- Moves freely and with pleasure and confidence in a range of ways, such as slithering, shuffling, rolling, crawling, walking, running, jumping, skipping, sliding and hopping.
- Draws lines and circles using gross motor movements.
- Uses one-handed tools and equipment, e.g. makes snips in paper with child scissors.

## 40–60 months

- Uses simple tools to effect changes to materials.
- Handles tools, objects, construction and malleable materials safely and with increasing control.

## Literacy

### Reading

### 30–50 months

- Enjoys rhyming and rhythmic activities.
- Shows awareness of rhyme and alliteration.
- Listens to and joins in with stories and poems, one to one and also in small groups.
- Joins in with repeated refrains and anticipates key events and phrases in rhymes and stories.
- Beginning to be aware of the way stories are structured.
- Suggests how the story might end.
- Describes main story settings, events and principal characters.

### 40–60 months

- Continues a rhyming string.
- Hears and says the initial sound in words.

## Mathematics

### Shape, space and measure

### 22–36 months

- Notices simple shapes and patterns in pictures.

### 30–50 months

- Shows an interest in shape and space by playing with shapes or making arrangements with objects.

## 40–60 months

- Uses familiar objects and common shapes to create and recreate patterns and build models.

# 🍃 *Understanding the world*

## *People and communities*

### 22–36 months

- In pretend play, imitates everyday actions and events from own family and cultural background, e.g. making and drinking tea.

## *The world*

### 30–50 months

- Comments and asks questions about aspects of their familiar world such as the place where they live or the natural world.
- Can talk about some of the things they have observed such as plants, animals, natural and found objects.

# 🎵 *Expressive arts and design*

## *Exploring and using media and materials*

### 8–20 months

- Imitates and improvises actions they have observed, e.g. clapping or waving.
- Begins to move to music, listen to or join in rhymes or songs.
- Notices and is interested in the effects of making movements which leave marks.

### 22–36 months

- Experiments with blocks, colours and marks.

### 30–50 months

- Enjoys joining in with dancing and ring games.
- Beginning to move rhythmically.

- Taps out simple repeated rhythms.
- Understands that they can use lines to enclose a space, and then begin to use these shapes to represent objects.
- Uses various construction materials.

## Being imaginative

### 16–26 months

- Expresses self through physical action and sound.
- Pretends that one object represents another, especially when objects have characteristics in common.

### 22–36 months

- Beginning to make-believe by pretending.

### 30–50 months

- Creates movement in response to music.
- Makes up rhythms.
- Uses available resources to create props to support role-play.
- Captures experiences and responses with a range of media, such as music, dance and paint and other materials or words.

### 40–60 months

- Chooses particular colours to use for a purpose.
- Introduces a storyline or narrative into their play.
- Plays alongside other children who are engaged in the same theme.

Development Matters in the Early Years Foundation Stage (EYFS): © Crown copyright 2012.

# 7 | July

British weather has a habit of surprising us, even in July! With this in mind, I've chosen festivals and events which highlight the changeable nature of the weather. Movement is key this month, getting out and about in the sunshine, or the rain, and making the most of it. The summer is a glorious time to introduce children to their environment and we shouldn't let the hint of a downpour dampen our spirits. The climate is changing, and so the world is changing too. It's important to introduce this idea at an early age. Even if young children do not understand the concept of climate change, they can see and experience weather patterns.

The cycle of life doesn't stop because it's wet. We adapt and learn to make the best of every eventuality. This is an important lesson for children and it's something we should embrace. Rain or shine, the wheel keeps turning, and there's lots of creative fun to be had!

## St Swithun's Day

St Swithun's Day falls on the 15th of July. St Swithun was a Saxon bishop from the ninth century. Legend has it that if it rains upon this day, then it will also rain for the next 40 days. This is apparently because it rained on the day they buried St Swithun's bones, and continued to do so for the next month. It's a unique way to forecast the weather, but also fun!

## Rainy-day fun

Start by explaining the origins of St Swithun's Day, and then ask the group what would happen if it rained for the next 40 days? What would this be like? Start by thinking about a physical representation of the rain, so use fingers, hands and arms to illustrate the rain coming down. Make the whooshing noise of the rain together, and add in other words and noises that demonstrate the sound it makes, so things like splishing, splashing, pitter pattering. Get the children on their feet, moving and shaking and making fluid movements to represent the water coming down. Ask them what they would do if it was pouring with rain. Perhaps they'd put up a huge umbrella. Maybe they would jump in puddles and splash about. Encourage them to have fun with this and let their imagination explore all the options of rainy-day fun.

When you've finished gather the group around you and begin to tell a story.

Say, 'Once upon a time, on St Swithun's Day, it began to rain. The sky turned black, and the clouds were grey, and the rain fell. It came down at first, in gentle drops, and then it got faster and faster, and heavier, until it was bouncing and sploshing on the ground. The children played in the puddles, they jumped and splashed about. But soon it became too wet for them to play out anymore. And still the rain came, faster and faster. So the children went back home, and they sat and watched from the window, and this is what they saw . . .'

Ask the group to think about what the children would see out of their window. Make it real by letting them look through any windows and describe the view. Encourage them to use descriptive words and connect ideas together. Ask them if they like the rain or if they prefer to stay dry. Then encourage them to draw pictures of a sunny and a rainy day. Highlight the differences between the two and the types of things you can do in different kinds of weather. Take them outside and ask them what they enjoy doing in the sun, and in the rain. Think about the difference in descriptive words and get little ones to repeat these words with you, and give them actions. Finally have a vote on who prefers which type of day and why. Start by saying 'I like rainy/sunny days because . . .' and make this a display that you can use to decorate the room. Take this a step further and think about 'windy days' or 'snowy days' and repeat the process.

### 💡 *Top tip*

Think about things that float on water, for example a boat, a surfboard or a raft. Ask older children to split into groups and create their own water transport. Encourage them to use their imagination, for example, they might take a colourful play mat and turn it into a magic carpet that floats on water, or an enchanted chair that skims the waves. Take this a step further and ask them to think about where they would go. Encourage them to get involved by creating story scenarios that they can act out.

## Water world

Introduce the idea of a watery world beneath the sea. If you like, you can base this on the mythical city of Atlantis, or make up somewhere new. What would it look like? Start by thinking about the main colours, and then think about what else you'd see. Encourage the children to draw pictures of this world. With very young children, use this as an opportunity for some colouring using crayons and paints. You can then use this made-up world as a setting for some storytelling, and link it to watery rhymes and songs.

## Asala – Dharma Day

Traditionally celebrated on the first full moon in July, Dharma Day is the anniversary of the start of the Buddha's teaching. It marks his first sermon, 'the wheel of truth', which happened after his enlightenment. It usually falls at the start of the rainy season in Nepal. It was believed to be a time when Buddha and his followers would pray and meditate. Because of the monsoon, they would take a break from travelling to spread his teachings, and instead shelter for three months. They used the time to seek further enlightenment. Today, the festival is about giving thanks for Buddha's teachings. Followers visit temples and sacred sites and pray for insights and inspiration.

## Build a shelter

Split the class into smaller groups and ask them to create a shelter just like Buddha. If it's possible you can do this activity outside, and use the landscape and the trees as a backdrop for your session. Start by explaining that Buddha and his followers would have looked for cover from the heavy rains in the trees, and that you are going to create your own tree house or shelter with things

you find in your surroundings. Encourage little ones to think about the shape of trees, and use pictures and words to describe them. If you're doing this inside, you can use chairs, building bricks, material, cardboard boxes and paper to create mini-shelters.

Finish with a game. Gather the group together. They're going to hold hands and dance around in a circular pattern until they hear the sound of the rain coming. You can make this noise yourself and encourage the group to join in with whooshing and sploshing noises. Get louder as the rain increases in power, and softer as it fades away. If you have some suitable music, use this to create the sound of the rain and vary the volume. Think about thunder too, what would this sound like? Take sheets of card, or drums, and encourage the children to make some noise and really get into the spirit of the weather. Now think about lightning, and how you might illustrate this. Use pieces of white material, or streamers, and get older children to imagine they're threads of lightning. How do they move through the air? What sort of patterns will they make? This activity works well with mixed-age groups, because you can ask the older children to be the bolts of lightning, and the younger ones to be the thunder and make some noise. See what kinds of patterns you can create, and get the children weaving between each other and navigating the space.

Finally tell them that when they hear the sound of thunder, they should run and take cover in one of the shelters they've made.

## Turning the wheel

On Dharma Day, followers are encouraged to 'turn the wheel' and go within and give thanks for Buddha's teachings. The wheel is a symbol that appears in many different spiritualities. Pagans often refer to the wheel of life, and the idea that it is ongoing, like a wheel continually turning. In reality, the wheel was a great invention, allowing us to move quickly and easily from A to B! As the wheel moves faster, so do we, going with the flow of motion.

Start by asking the group to think about the shape of the wheel and how it moves. You might want to start with a rhyme or song, like 'the wheels on the bus', just to get them into the spirit of exercise! Now, encourage them to think about objects with wheels and come up with a list. Ask them to draw pictures of all the different inventions that have wheels; this can include the Ferris wheel, the spinning wheel in the playground, cars, buses, lorries, tractors, bikes and fire engines. In groups play counting games by asking them to count how many wheels they see in the pictures. Which object has more wheels? Which has the biggest wheel? Which has the smallest? Could they add more wheels, and how many wheels would that make? Use toys with wheels to illustrate how they move and encourage younger children to play with them, moving them around the room.

With older children, ask them to think about how fast a wheel turns, when it's going up and down hill, and what about the size of the wheel? If it's small, does it go faster?

## Top tip

Get the group together and ask them to come up with a counting rhyme that includes wheels. So you might start by saying, 'One wheel, two wheels, three wheels, four, how many wheels do you see on the floor? Five wheels, six wheels, seven or more, how do they move when they're on the floor?'

Then using the pictures they've drawn, point to a picture of a car, and encourage them to count the wheels with you. Move on to a picture of a big wheel, and repeat the phrase together. Go around the room using all of the pictures, and encouraging the group to join in with a ditty whilst counting at the same time. If you prefer you can use models of cars and lorries to do the same thing, or even picture books.

# Ramadan

This is the month when Muslims fast during daylight hours. It relates to the ninth month of the Muslim calendar and the night that the Qur'an was revealed to the prophet Muhammad. It is also the time when Muslims believe that the gates of heaven are open and the gates of hell closed, with all of the devils chained up. Because of this followers believe it is easier to do good during this month, as there is no temptation. Although it's hard to ascertain the exact date when the Qur'an was first read, it is thought to be one of the last 10 nights of Ramadan. Because of this, Muslims attempt to read as much of the Qur'an as they can at this time. They fast in an attempt to show self-discipline in all areas of their life.

## Reading quests

This is something you can do with older children during the month of Ramadan. Set up a reading quest. The idea is that they have to split into teams and read as many picture books as they can in a session. Encourage them to pick their favourites and talk about why they enjoyed them. Did they learn anything from the book? Did they particularly like the pictures? Also ask them to have a go at writing any new words that they have learnt. Set some time aside during each session for them to have a go at reading aloud. By the end of the month you can have a mammoth 'read out loud' session and they can pick a book and read a page from it.

# Development matters covered

Below you will find a list of key development matters covered in the activities above.

## Communication and language

### Listening and attention

#### 8–20 months

- Has a strong exploratory impulse.
- Concentrates intently on an object or activity of own choosing for short periods.
- Moves whole body to enjoyable sounds, such as music or a regular beat.
- Pays attention to dominant stimulus – easily distracted by noises or other people talking.

#### 16–26 months

- Listens to and enjoys rhythmic patterns in rhymes and stories.
- Enjoys rhymes and demonstrates listening by trying to join in with actions or vocalisation.

#### 22–36 months

- Listens with interest to the noises adults make when they read stories.
- Shows interest in play with sounds, songs and rhymes.

#### 30–50 months

- Listens to others one to one or in small groups, when conversation interests them.
- Joins in with repeated refrains and anticipates key events and phrases in rhymes and stories.

### Understanding

#### 8–20 months

- Developing the ability to follow others' body language, including pointing and gesture.

## 16–26 months

- Understands simple sentences, e.g. 'Throw the ball.'

## 22–36 months

- Understands more complex sentences, e.g. 'Put your toys away and then we'll read a book.'
- Understands 'who', 'what', 'where' in simple questions, e.g. Who's that/who can? What's that? Where is . . .?

## 30–50 months

- Understands use of objects, e.g. 'What do we use to cut things?'
- Responds to simple instructions, e.g. to get or put away an object.

## 40–60 months

- Able to follow a story without pictures or props.
- Listens and responds to ideas expressed by others in conversation or discussion.

### *Speaking*

## 8–20 months

- Uses sounds in play, e.g. 'brrrm' for toy car.
- Uses single words.
- Frequently imitates words and sounds.

## 16–26 months

- Beginning to ask simple questions.
- Beginning to talk about people and things that are not present.

## 22–36 months

- Uses language as a powerful means of widening contacts, sharing feelings, experiences and thoughts.

## 30–50 months

- Uses talk to connect ideas, explain what is happening and anticipate what might happen next, recall and relive past experiences.
- Questions why things happen and gives explanations. Asks e.g. who, what, when, how.

## 40–60 months

- Extends vocabulary, especially by grouping and naming, exploring the meaning and sounds of new words.
- Uses language to imagine and recreate roles and experiences in play situations.

## Physical development

### Moving and handling

## 8–20 months

- Picks up small objects between thumb and fingers.
- Enjoys the sensory experience of making marks in damp sand, paste or paint.
- Holds pen or crayon using a whole hand (palmar) grasp and makes random marks with different strokes.

## 22–36 months

- Shows control in holding and using jugs to pour, hammers, books and mark-making tools.
- Beginning to use three fingers (tripod grip) to hold writing tools.
- Imitates drawing simple shapes such as circles and lines.

## 30–50 months

- Draws lines and circles using gross motor movements.
- Uses one-handed tools and equipment, e.g. makes snips in paper with child scissors.

## 40–60 months

- Uses simple tools to effect changes to materials.
- Handles tools, objects, construction and malleable materials safely and with increasing control.

# Literacy

## Reading

### 16–26 months

- Interested in books and rhymes and may have favourites.

### 22–36 months

- Has some favourite stories, rhymes, songs, poems or jingles.
- Repeats words or phrases from familiar stories.

### 30–50 months

- Enjoys rhyming and rhythmic activities.
- Shows awareness of rhyme and alliteration.
- Listens to and joins in with stories and poems, one to one and also in small groups.
- Joins in with repeated refrains and anticipates key events and phrases in rhymes and stories.
- Beginning to be aware of the way stories are structured.
- Suggests how the story might end.
- Describes main story settings, events and principal characters.

### 40–60 months

- Continues a rhyming string.
- Hears and says the initial sound in words.

# Mathematics

## Numbers

### 16–26 months

- Says some counting words randomly.

### 22–36 months

- Recites some number names in sequence.

## 30–50 months

- Uses some number names and number language spontaneously.
- Uses some number names accurately in play.
- Recites numbers in order to 10.
- Knows that numbers identify how many objects are in a set.

## 40–60 months

- Counts actions or objects which cannot be moved.
- Counts objects to 10, and beginning to count beyond 10.

### *Shape, space and measure*

## 22–36 months

- Notices simple shapes and patterns in pictures.

## 30–50 months

- Shows an interest in shape and space by playing with shapes or making arrangements with objects.

## 40–60 months

- Uses familiar objects and common shapes to create and recreate patterns and build models.

# Understanding the world

### *The world*

## 30–50 months

- Comments and asks questions about aspects of their familiar world such as the place where they live or the natural world.
- Can talk about some of the things they have observed, such as plants, animals, natural and found objects.

## 🎵 *Expressive arts and design*

### *Exploring and using media and materials*

#### 8–20 months

- Imitates and improvises actions they have observed, e.g. clapping or waving.
- Begins to move to music, listen to or join in rhymes or songs.
- Notices and is interested in the effects of making movements which leave marks.

#### 22–36 months

- Experiments with blocks, colours and marks.

#### 30–50 months

- Enjoys joining in with dancing and ring games.
- Beginning to move rhythmically.
- Taps out simple repeated rhythms.
- Understands that they can use lines to enclose a space, and then begin to use these shapes to represent objects.
- Uses various construction materials.

### *Being imaginative*

#### 16–26 months

- Expresses self through physical action and sound.
- Pretends that one object represents another, especially when objects have characteristics in common.

#### 22–36 months

- Beginning to make-believe by pretending.

#### 30–50 months

- Creates movement in response to music.
- Makes up rhythms.

- Uses available resources to create props to support role-play.
- Captures experiences and responses with a range of media, such as music, dance and paint and other materials or words.

## 40–60 months

- Chooses particular colours to use for a purpose.
- Introduces a storyline or narrative into their play.
- Plays alongside other children who are engaged in the same theme.

Development Matters in the Early Years Foundation Stage (EYFS): © Crown copyright 2012.

# 8 | August

Summer has arrived, in a flurry of colour, heat and vibrant activity. If we marked the passing year by shades, then this month would be pillar-box red and amber orange, with a splash of zingy lemon freshness. We often ignore the value of colour in our life, letting the palette of every day wash over us. It's interesting then that colours play a big part in celebrations around the world. We use colour to symbolise the spirit of the event, and show how we feel. It captures the imagination and helps us connect to the energy behind the festivity. Ribbons are also a useful tool and are often tied together to represent unity, the combination of colours symbolising the joining together of ideas. With this in mind, I have created activities that use the power of colour to illustrate a point and the movement and flexibility of ribbons. It's important to show children how to appreciate this medium and use simple crafting skills to connect and share their emotions and beliefs with others.

## Lammas

Our Celtic ancestors celebrated Lammas on the 1st of August. The name itself is medieval and means 'loaf mass' as it was the time when the first grains of the harvest were collected and baked as bread. Lammas is a time to give thanks for the harvest and reap the rewards of the seeds sown earlier in the year. People would bake bread and leave it upon church altars in worship and there was usually a great feast to mark the event. In Irish Gaelic, the feast had a different name, Lughnasadh, and it was a celebration of the sun god Lugh, and his sacrifice. It was believed that at this time each year he would die and pour all his energy into the grain so that his people could eat. In effect this represented the end of summer and the beginning of autumn. The idea was that Lugh would be reborn again in spring, and so the circle of life would continue. People would dress up in brightly coloured clothes. They would dance with ribbons and perform special ceremonies to mark the passing of the sun. Corn dollies were also popular and made to represent the Corn Goddess. It was believed that she lived in the fields of corn, and was responsible for blessing their growth. To keep her spirit alive, they would retain some of the corn picked and make small dolls to play with until the new crop of corn was planted.

## Lammas dance

The colours associated with Lammas are yellow, orange, gold and red, all vibrant shades that represent the sun. Start by asking the children what different colours they think of when they think about the sun. To help, get paints and crayons out and let them experiment, making patterns with these colours on paper.

Explain that, a long time ago, people would have danced with ribbons in these colours to honour the power of the sun. In groups you're going to create ceremonial sticks and decorations that you can use in a sun dance. Gather together ribbons, material, tissue paper, cardboard, toilet rolls and anything that you can use to make these items. Start by showing the group how to tape together the toilet rolls to form a stick that they can wave about. Encourage them to decorate the stick by painting, or covering with coloured paper and glitter. Next take the ribbons, and tape them to the end of the stick. Have fun with this and use different kinds of material, so you might want to include streamers, feathers and tissue paper. The idea is that when you wave the stick about you can create interesting patterns and sounds by using lots of different textures.

Encourage the children to have a go at making shapes in the air. So start by making circle patterns for the sun, then move on to crosses, squares and any other kind of patterns you can think of. Put some music on and get the children to wave their stick in time with the beat. Have fun and come up with a sun dance. So think about what your feet might be doing at the same time. Perhaps you could tap out a rhythm or rock back and forth in time with the music. Put words to this, so you might repeat something simple to encourage actions, like, 'Hooray for the sun, it lives in the sky. Look up at its light and wave your hands high! Sway to the left, sway to the right, jump up and down with all of your might!'

When you're ready, start to move around the room in a procession. Get the children to copy your actions and see if they can keep up.

Split older children into pairs and ask them to create their own Lammas sun dance. They can use the movements that you've already practised and come up with new ones. If they want, they can put words to the dance, or just follow the music.

Create a sun spot in the centre of the room. You can do this by using carefully positioned mats, or drawing and painting a large orange dot on a sheet of paper. You could also mark out the spot using stones. This is going to be the stage. Give every pair a chance to perform their sun dance to the rest of the group and ask for feedback.

## Corn dolly capers

Making corn dollies can be a fiddly business, especially with small children, but it's worth having a go for the end result. Practise making them yourself first, so that you know what to do, then you can show the children.

You will need some corn husks which have been soaked for a few hours to make them soft and pliable. You will also need some thread and some cotton wool balls.

1.  Take a strip of the husk and fold it in half, place a couple of cotton wool balls in between and then twist the husk around these to create a head shape. Leave some of the husk hanging down to create a body.

2.  To make arms, take another strip of husk, and tie near both ends to create hands. Slip this husk between the husk that forms the torso to create arms that stick out. You may want to insert another cotton ball at this point to pad the body out.

3.  Add in some more stalks of corn and tie at the waist to create a skirt for your dolly. You may need to trim these to create the shape you want.

4.  When you've finished, leave the doll to dry and then she's ready for decorating. Some people prefer to leave their corn dollies plain, but it's a great idea to encourage the children to personalise them. You can give them hair by using wool, and clothes, by using up bits of material.

If you prefer, you can take an easier option and use play dough to sculpt a dolly shape. Get into smaller groups and work together on this. Mould the dough into the shape of a corn dolly. Use a round ball for the head, a triangular shape for the body, and two smaller sausage pieces for arms that stick out. Encourage little ones to think about what else they need to create the dolly, so buttons for eyes, a mouth, perhaps some hair? Explain that their ancestors would have made these dolls out of strands of corn, and that they believed that they were magic.

Ask little ones to think of a name for their doll. Where does she live, and what magic power does she have? Encourage them to develop this into a story, and use paper and crayons to illustrate this. Ask them questions like, what does she like to eat? Who does she like to play with, or where does she sleep at night? Encourage them to make corn dolly friends and props from the play dough that they can use in a short tale about their dolly. Give each group the chance to share their tales, and ask them questions.

# Raksha Bandhan

This Hindu festival celebrates the bond between brother and sister and is often abbreviated to Rakhi. It's a festival of love and brotherhood during which sisters will tie a rakhi, which is a bracelet made of threads of red and gold, around their brother's wrist. This represents the ties between them, and the love they share. Today rakhis can be shared with friends, to celebrate the relationship. When a rakhi is tied, a wish for love and happiness is made, often in the form of a chant or prayer. The bracelet is said to protect its wearer for the following year. After the rakhi has been tied, the giver may place a sweet in the recipient's mouth, and the wearer may give a gift of money to the other person.

## *Bracelet bonding*

Split the group into pairs and encourage them to make their own rakhi bracelet. Explain where the idea comes from and gather together coloured string, ribbons, paper and anything that can be tied around the wrist to form a bracelet. Think about the colours used traditionally and talk about what they mean. So, for example, what does the colour red remind them of? What other things are red? Do they like the colour? How does it make them

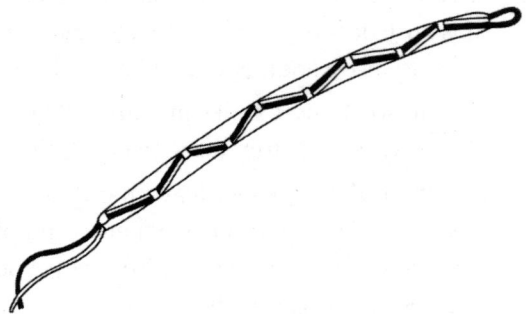

feel? What about gold? Do they like it, and if so, why? Ask them to come up with words associated with the colours, and once you have a list, create a rhyme or chant together. Once they have created their rakhi bracelet, they should exchange it with their partner. Older children might want to make a wish or say a simple rhyme.

Finish the activity by coming together in a larger group to create a friendship rhyme. Choose something easy that you can repeat and put actions to. So, something like, 'We are friends, we have fun. We sing and we dance. We jump up and down and we wave our hands. We spin round and round, stretch our arms in the air. Together we are friends. We play and share.'

Repeat the rhyme in a circle, including the actions and make it fun, by changing the speed, and increasing volume.

## Top tip

Ask older children to think about their relationships. Get them to draw a picture of themselves with their best friend. As they do this encourage them to talk about their friendship. Why do they like this person? What kind of things do they like to do together? Ask them to write a couple of sentences to go with the picture. Something simple like, 'This is my friend Alice, we like to play together on the swings.' When they've finished get the group into a circle and give everyone the chance to share their pictures and read their sentences.

### Parent fun

Encourage the children to make rakhi bracelets for the rest of the family using different coloured ribbons. Get the parents involved in picking colours and tying the bracelets together.

# Eid

This marks the end of the month of fasting for the Muslim faith. (Dates may vary, and sometimes this festival falls in July.) It's an auspicious time, and it's heralded by the sight of the first new moon. Muslims celebrate by decorating their homes and dressing up in their best clothes. They have a great feast, the first served during the day after Ramadan. It's a time to give thanks to Allah for helping them stay strong throughout their fasting. It's also a time for forgiveness.

### 'Thankful' tea party

Throw a tea party with a twist, and encourage the children to give thanks for all the good things in their life. Keep it simple, and include a clapping exercise, as a way of applauding all the things they are thankful for. So you might start by saying 'We are thankful for the food', then get everyone clapping their hands. Go through a list of other things you could be thankful for, so you might say:

> We are thankful for:
> Each other
> Mummy and daddy
> Being able to play
> Where we live
> Our fingers
> Our toes
> Our eyes
> Our nose

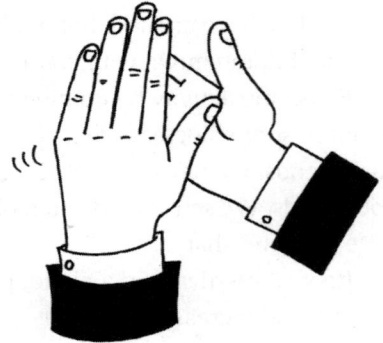

Remember to applaud each item on the list, and give older children the opportunity to come up with anything they're thankful for, for example a special toy or a pet, or something else that makes them happy.

## Development matters covered

Below you will find a list of key development matters covered in the activities above.

### Communication and language

*Listening and attention*

8–20 months

- Has a strong exploratory impulse.
- Moves whole body to enjoyable sounds, such as music or a regular beat.
- Pays attention to dominant stimulus – easily distracted by noises or other people talking.

## 16–26 months

- Listens to and enjoys rhythmic patterns in rhymes and stories.
- Enjoys rhymes and demonstrates listening by trying to join in with actions or vocalisation.

## 22–36 months

- Listens with interest to the noises adults make when they read stories.
- Shows interest in play with sounds, songs and rhymes.

## 30–50 months

- Listens to others one to one or in small groups, when conversation interests them.
- Joins in with repeated refrains and anticipates key events and phrases in rhymes and stories.

## *Understanding*

## 8–20 months

- Developing the ability to follow others' body language, including pointing and gesture.

## 16–26 months

- Understands simple sentences, e.g. 'Throw the ball.'

## 22–36 months

- Understands more complex sentences, e.g. 'Put your toys away and then we'll read a book.'
- Understands 'who', 'what', 'where' in simple questions, e.g. Who's that/who can? What's that? Where is . . .?

## 30–50 months

- Understands use of objects, e.g. 'What do we use to cut things?'
- Responds to simple instructions, e.g. to get or put away an object.

## 40–60 months

- Able to follow a story without pictures or props.
- Listens and responds to ideas expressed by others in conversation or discussion.

## Speaking

### 8–20 months

- Uses sounds in play, e.g. 'brrrm' for toy car.
- Uses single words.
- Frequently imitates words and sounds.

### 16–26 months

- Beginning to ask simple questions.
- Beginning to talk about people and things that are not present.

### 22–36 months

- Uses language as a powerful means of widening contacts, sharing feelings, experiences and thoughts.

### 30–50 months

- Uses talk to connect ideas, explain what is happening and anticipate what might happen next, recall and relive past experiences.
- Questions why things happen and gives explanations. Asks e.g. who, what, when, how.

### 40–60 months

- Extends vocabulary, especially by grouping and naming, exploring the meaning and sounds of new words.
- Uses language to imagine and recreate roles and experiences in play situations.

## Physical development

### Moving and handling

### 8–20 months

- Picks up small objects between thumb and fingers.
- Enjoys the sensory experience of making marks in damp sand, paste or paint.
- Holds pen or crayon using a whole hand (palmar) grasp and makes random marks with different strokes.
- Crawls, bottom shuffles or rolls continuously to move around.

## 16–26 months

- Makes connections between their movement and the marks they make.

## 22–36 months

- Shows control in holding and using jugs to pour, hammers, books and mark-making tools.
- Beginning to use three fingers (tripod grip) to hold writing tools.
- Imitates drawing simple shapes such as circles and lines.

## 30–50 months

- Draws lines and circles using gross motor movements.
- Uses one-handed tools and equipment, e.g. makes snips in paper with child scissors.
- Moves freely and with pleasure and confidence in a range of ways, such as slithering, shuffling, rolling, crawling, walking, running, jumping, skipping, sliding and hopping.

## 40–60 months

- Uses simple tools to effect changes to materials.
- Handles tools, objects, construction and malleable materials safely and with increasing control.
- Negotiates space successfully when playing racing and chasing games with other children, adjusting speed or changing direction to avoid obstacles.
- Shows increasing control over an object in pushing, patting, throwing, catching or kicking it.

# 📖 *Literacy*

## *Reading*

## 30–50 months

- Enjoys rhyming and rhythmic activities.
- Shows awareness of rhyme and alliteration.
- Listens to and joins in with stories and poems, one to one and also in small groups.
- Joins in with repeated refrains and anticipates key events and phrases in rhymes and stories.

## 40–60 months

- Continues a rhyming string.
- Hears and says the initial sound in words.

# Mathematics

## Shape, space and measure

### 22–36 months

- Notices simple shapes and patterns in pictures.

### 30–50 months

- Shows an interest in shape and space by playing with shapes or making arrangements with objects.

### 40–60 months

- Uses familiar objects and common shapes to create and recreate patterns and build models.

# Understanding the world

## People and communities

### 16–26 months

- Is curious about people and shows interest in stories about themselves and their family.
- Enjoys pictures and stories about themselves, their families and other people.

### 22–36 months

- Has a sense of own immediate family and relations.

### 30–50 months

- Shows interest in the lives of people who are familiar to them.
- Remembers and talks about significant events in their own experience.
- Recognises and describes special times or events for family or friends.

## 40–60 months

- Enjoys joining in with family customs and routines.

# 🎵 *Expressive arts and design*

## *Exploring and using media and materials*

### 8–20 months

- Imitates and improvises actions they have observed, e.g. clapping or waving.
- Begins to move to music, listen to or join in rhymes or songs.
- Notices and is interested in the effects of making movements which leave marks.
- Explores and experiments with a range of media through sensory exploration, and using whole body.

### 22–36 months

- Experiments with blocks, colours and marks.
- Joins in singing favourite songs.
- Creates sounds by banging, shaking, tapping or blowing.

### 30–50 months

- Enjoys joining in with dancing and ring games.
- Beginning to move rhythmically.
- Taps out simple repeated rhythms.
- Understands that they can use lines to enclose a space, and then begin to use these shapes to represent objects.
- Uses various construction materials

## *Being imaginative*

### 16–26 months

- Expresses self through physical action and sound.
- Pretends that one object represents another, especially when objects have characteristics in common.

### 22–36 months

- Beginning to make-believe by pretending.

## 30–50 months

- Creates movement in response to music.
- Makes up rhythms.
- Uses available resources to create props to support role-play.
- Captures experiences and responses with a range of media, such as music, dance and paint and other materials or words.

## 40–60 months

- Chooses particular colours to use for a purpose.
- Introduces a storyline or narrative into their play.
- Plays alongside other children who are engaged in the same theme.

Development Matters in the Early Years Foundation Stage (EYFS): © Crown copyright 2012.

# 9 | September

Creative play is an essential element in learning. Through this we can help young children explore and learn for themselves by engaging them in tasks that make the experience real. It's been said that, to develop empathy, you must walk a mile in another's shoes. It helps us understand the world around us, if we can put ourselves in different situations, and think what we might learn from each experience. This is something we do naturally as we get older, and we can encourage children to get into the habit of using this life skill from an early age.

Using pictures, sounds and movement, we can set the scene and give children the perfect platform for experimentation. Rather than introducing them to the celebration, we choose a central character that links into the event and ask them to imagine that they are this character. Young children will not understand this concept, but they can still have fun dressing up and exploring sound and movement in pretend play. With older children we can encourage them to form their own opinions. Ask them to work together and plan a structure for their ideas using lists and pictures. Get them thinking creatively, but, most importantly, having fun as they take on new roles and engage with characters from each event.

## Michaelmas – 29th September

Michaelmas is the feast of St Michael, the Archangel who threw Satan to earth. He is the warrior Archangel and known for his incredible strength and power. Because this celebration falls near the equinox, on the 29th of September, it's linked to the beginning of autumn and the shortening of days. It's also the time when the harvest was over, and the bailiff of the manor would do his accounts for the year, setting everything in order for winter. Goose is most commonly eaten at this celebration.

Michael is the angel of protection and has a reputation for fighting evil. He is often pictured with a sword and a shield, which symbolise his ability to cut away things we no longer need and offer protection. Spiritually he is linked to the colour blue. He is often represented in pictures as a mighty angel, with huge white wings.

## Fly away

Start by introducing the group to the Archangel Michael. You might want to show them pictures, and explain a little about him and the festival of Michaelmas. Talk about his strength and power. Ask them to think about angels, where do they live, what do they look like, how do they move, what are their names? This will encourage the flow of ideas. Tell them that they are all going to be angels for the day. They must start by making a pair of wings that they can carry, or wear. So they might want to use paper and draw wings that they can cut out and wave, or drape a piece of cloth over their shoulders and pretend they have wings. This is an opportunity for them to get creative and decorate their wings with whatever they have to hand. Ask them to think about other props that they might use, for example they might want a golden halo, or a trumpet. Also get them to create an angel name for themselves; they can either use their own name or come up with a new one. Help them to make a badge which they can wear to say who they are.

Next encourage them to use their wings and fly around the room. What kind of movements should they make? What sorts of words describe how angels fly? Get a rhythmic chant going, so you might say, 'With my wings I flap and wave, I swirl and twirl, I sway and swoop, I stretch up and down, I flutter and soar.'

Think about the actions that go with these words and get them to join in. Create a pattern on the floor that you can follow, and imagine you're flying through the sky. If you have access to some space outside, use this, and plot a route using angel markers. Encourage them to think about other things that are in the sky. So you might want to plot out clouds that they can jump on.

### Top tip

With older children split them into smaller groups and ask them to come up with a story which starts 'If I was an angel for a day, I would . . .' Together they must come up with an 'angel manifesto' of the kind of things that they would do. Encourage them to think about what an angel is, and how it might do good and help others. Finally, give each group a turn in the spotlight, so they can wear their angel wings, and share their ideas.

# Ganesh Chaturthi

This is an important date for the Hindu faith, although it varies depending on when the waxing moon falls. It's the birthday of Ganesh, the elephant-headed god, and a time when Hindus celebrate new beginnings, for example getting married, moving house. Ganesh is the god of success and wisdom and he blesses every new beginning with his benevolence. During the festival idols of the god are created and placed on display with colourful fresh flowers and sweet treats. On the final day of the celebration there is a procession and the idols are carried to nearby rivers or lakes and immersed in the water. This marks the festival coming to an end. Followers dance and sing and raise their voices in worship to urge the god to make a swift return next year and bring them success.

## Animal magic

Introduce the group to a range of different types of animals from around the world by using pictures, or picture books as prompts. Start with animals that they may already have encountered, and then move on to some of the more exotic creatures. Think of the god Ganesh, who had an elephant's head. You're going to create a selection of different animal masks using paper, crayons and any other tools, which the children can wear to become the animal. The idea is that this will eventually develop into a fun game that you can play in smaller groups.

Once they've created the masks, get them to play and become the animal by thinking about how it might move, what sounds it makes. Encourage them to swap masks so that they can experience the differences between creatures and the way they act.

## Top tip

Get older children more involved by encouraging them to tell a story about their chosen animal. They can do this using pictures to illustrate what happens. So first of all they should think about the setting for their story: where does their creature live? Allow them a set amount of time to get their picture finished, then blow a whistle and tell them that it's time for some animal magic. They should leave their masks together with the first picture in the centre of the room. They must then pick a new mask. This time they're going to think about the next stage in the story with this new animal. So what does it do for breakfast? Where does it go? What does it eat? Again get them to draw a quick picture. Blow the whistle and once again ask them to leave their pictures and mask and choose a new animal. This time you could ask them to draw their animal doing its favourite thing, which could be sleeping, climbing trees, swimming, jumping. Encourage them to be creative, so if they think that an elephant likes reading the newspaper in the morning, then ask them to draw a picture of this! Get the group to mix it up as they think about each animal. It doesn't matter how silly it sounds, encourage them to create fun activities and pictures which will ultimately become a short narrative of its daily habits.

When everyone has had a few turns, you should have a series of pictures for each animal. Gather them together, and in a larger group begin telling each story. Pick someone to wear the animal mask, and then encourage the rest of the group to join in with the telling of the tale, picking out interesting-sounding words and actions. Make this an exercise in group storytelling, and invite new ideas for what might happen next.

When you've finished use the pictures and masks to create a colourful wall display of animal life.

## *Totem power*

The symbol of the elephant head gives Ganesh great power, wisdom and strength, just like the animal that it represents. This kind of association is commonplace around the world as animals are often linked to different skills and strengths. Many spiritual and religious groups revere them for their powers, and work with them in celebration and worship. Every creature is unique and has a special gift and this is an important lesson in life. Help young children understand the beauty of the natural world by encouraging them to look at wildlife in a different way. Help them to appreciate and celebrate the differences in the species, and this in turn will help them embrace the differences in each other.

Start by splitting them into smaller groups. Give each one an animal to work with. Use a range of different creatures from around the world, but also include those that you would find here in the UK. By providing a wide selection of animals, you're illustrating that everyone has a role to play, and by using creatures that are already familiar, you're helping them to develop respect and appreciation for those that are less common.

To help with this exercise provide pictures, stories, poems and models of the animals. Help each group use these to find out as much as they can about their allotted creature, and what its particular gift or strength is. Once they have decided what it is that they like about this animal, they must put together a simple rhyme. For example, if they chose the fox, they might say:

We like fox because he's furry and red. We like fox because he uses his head. We like fox because you can see him on the street. We like fox because he's quick on his feet.

Encourage the younger children to put actions to the rhyme and think of it like a performance that they can share with the rest of the group.

Get them involved in creating pictures and props that they can use in their performance.

> ## Top tip
>
> Young children will not understand the differences between the animals, but they are starting to pick up on sounds and movements. So give them a combination of sounds and actions, to help them identify each animal. For example, you might make a growling noise for a tiger and use your hands in a clawing motion. You might make a hooting noise for an owl and stretch your arms out at the sides as if you're flying. Get the group to join in with each movement and sound, and then turn it into a game, by asking them to guess which animal you're mimicking.
>
> To finish choose one of the animals that you've been using and create a simple springboard story. If it helps, use an existing tale or picture book. For example, *The Tiger Who Came to Tea* is a great starting point, because you can set the scene and use any animal you like.
>
> > Lucy was sitting at the table ready for tea. She was very hungry. All of sudden there was a loud knock at the door – knock, knock, knock.
> > 'Who's that mummy?' Lucy asked. 'Let's go and see.' Mummy said.
> > Together they opened the door, and there stood . . .
>
> At this point you can get the children to shout out their favourite animal, or choose one for them. Then proceed with the tale by asking them what happened next.

# Autumn equinox

Otherwise known as Mabon, this pagan festival celebrates the harvest and is a time to give thanks for the crops. It falls around the 22nd of the month, and it marks a time when both day and night are of equal length. Pagans use this festival to reflect upon the past year. It represents the cycle of life, and the changing seasons, as summer moves into autumn and winter. Pagans believe that the Sun God is now passing, flowing into the arms of the goddess and winter time. This festival is about embracing the balance between light and dark and giving thanks for all the good things in our lives.

## Mabon altar

The Celts would have celebrated Mabon with a great feast. It is also likely that they would have created a special altar in their homes as a way of marking this festival. Follow suit by dedicating an area of the room to Mabon and creating your own special altar. Traditionally this altar would be adorned with things from nature – fruit, seeds, acorns, berries and leaves. Encourage the children to bring some of these items in and place them on the altar. Make it as colourful as possible and bring the outside in by gathering twigs, plants, leaves and stones. Ask the group to make pictures and collages using some of the items that they have collected. The idea is to make the display a wonderful riot of colour and texture!

### Top tip

Older children will understand a little more about the concept of the harvest and giving thanks for the good things in their life. Encourage them to write a Mabon poem which talks about some of the things that they enjoy and appreciate. Make it simple by starting with key words for things, then think about other words that add to the description. Encourage them to think about how things sound together by making interesting rhyming sentences. Display any poetic offerings on the Mabon altar for everyone to see.

# Development matters covered

Below you will find a list of key development matters covered in the activities above.

## Communication and language

### Listening and attention

#### 16–26 months

* Listens to and enjoys rhythmic patterns in rhymes and stories.
* Enjoys rhymes and demonstrates listening by trying to join in with actions or vocalisations.

## 22–36 months

- Listens with interest to the noises adults make when they read stories.
- Recognises and responds to many familiar sounds, e.g. turning to a knock on the door, looking at or going to the door.
- Shows interest in play with sounds, songs and rhymes.

## 30–50 months

- Listens to stories with increasing attention and recall.
- Joins in with repeated refrains and anticipates key events and phrases in rhymes and stories.

### Speaking

## 22–36 months

- Learns new words very rapidly and is able to use them in communicating.

## 30–50 months

- Uses intonation, rhythm and phrasing to make the meaning clear to others.

# Physical development

### Moving and handling

## 30–50 months

- Moves freely and with pleasure and confidence in a range of ways, such as slithering, shuffling, rolling, crawling, walking, running, jumping, skipping, sliding and hopping.
- Uses one-handed tools and equipment, e.g. makes snips in paper with scissors.

## 40–60 months

- Negotiates space successfully when playing racing and chasing games with other children, adjusting speed or changing direction to avoid obstacles.
- Uses simple tools to effect changes to materials.

## Literacy

### Reading

#### 30–50 months

- Enjoys rhyming and rhythmic activities.
- Listens to and joins in with stories and poems, one to one and also in small groups.
- Joins in with repeated refrains and anticipates key events and phrases in rhymes and stories.

### Writing

#### 30–50 months

- Sometimes gives meaning to marks as they draw and paint.
- Ascribes meanings to marks that they see in different places.

#### 40–60 months

- Attempts to write short sentences in meaningful contexts.
- Suggests how a story might end.
- Describes main story settings, events and characters.
- Gives meaning to marks they make as they draw, write and paint.

## Understanding the world

### The world

#### 22–36 months

- Notices detailed features of objects in their environment.

#### 30–50 months

- Comments and asks questions about aspects of their familiar world such as the place where they live or the natural world.
- Can talk about some of the things they have observed such as plants, animals, natural and found objects.

## 🎵 *Expressive arts and design*

### *Exploring and using media and materials*

#### 30–50 months

- Beginning to move rhythmically.
- Explores and learns how sounds can be changed.

### *Being imaginative*

#### 30–50 months

- Uses available resources to create props to support role-play.
- Captures experiences and responses with a range of media, such as music, dance and paint and other materials or words.

#### 40–60 months

- Plays cooperatively as part of a group to develop and act out a narrative.

Development Matters in the Early Years Foundation Stage (EYFS): © Crown copyright 2012.

# 10 | October

October offers an array of interesting festivals which provide the opportunity to get practical and construct something. There's something special about using your hands to form something out of nothing. Working with the surroundings and using them to produce something that helps to connect us to the world and the beliefs of others gives us a greater understanding of life. So it makes sense that when we get children involved in the practical construction of an object, they will gain a lot. Not only do they learn about the subject, but they use a range of creative skills and work together to produce the end result. Provide a narrative structure to help them piece their ideas together and you have a recipe for lots of fun!

## Sukkot

This Jewish festival, which tends to fall at the beginning of October, celebrates the years that the Jews spent in the desert during their journey to the promised land. The idea is that, despite their extreme conditions, God looked after and supported them. This festival gives thanks for God's love and embraces the idea that he is always there to provide help and comfort. Sukkot is also known as the Feast of the Tabernacles. The word Sukkot means 'huts' and one of the rituals carried out to celebrate this festival is the building of a hut using a palm branch, a citron and wood from the myrtle and the willow tree. This hut can be built in the garden, and Jewish people often sit in it to eat their meals and pray. The hut should be flimsy, as this supports the idea that when we don't have much, we still have God. We are still close to him, and can see and feel him by looking up into the sky. Today, it isn't always possible to build a hut, so many Jews celebrate by waving palm, myrtle or willow branches.

## Build a den

One of the best ways to introduce children to this festival is to encourage them to build a den or hut using materials that they can gather outside. Like the Sukkot that the Jewish people construct, these don't have to be particularly stable or secure (you're not going to encourage the children to climb them); the idea is that they collect materials and see how they might fit together to make a structure by using their imagination. Use whatever you have to hand: twigs, leaves, cardboard and paper make good starting materials. If you don't have access to wood or leaves, get the children to draw these things on to card or paper, or use cardboard boxes of different shapes and sizes. Explain that building a hut is part of the celebration for this festival, and also lots of fun. If you can, take the children outside and encourage them to look up at the sky. What do they see? Help them to imagine what it would be like to live in a wooden hut beneath the sky. Sit in a circle and create a song to celebrate the outside world. Start with something simple like, 'When I look around I see . . .' and then ask the children to fill in the gaps taking inspiration from their surroundings. Encourage them to add more description to their answers, and repeat the phrase until it becomes a chant with actions and movement.

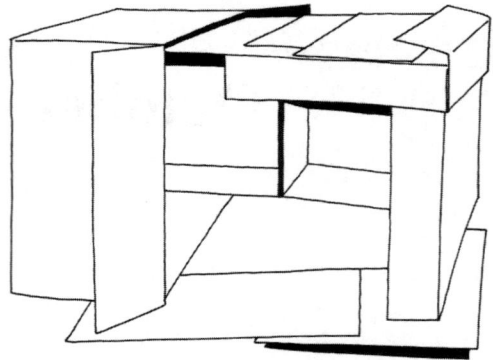

Take this a step further, and ask them to create a collage of pictures, using materials from their environment. Include lots of different textures that they can feel and experiment with. Twigs, sticks, grass and leaves are all good choices and easy to find. Talk about the different types of colours they might use and ask them to create a picture of what they might see if they lived in a hut outside.

# Samhain – 31st October

An ancient Celtic festival, Samhain, pronounced 'sow-inn', marks the end of summer and the final harvest. The Celts believed that, on this night, the veil between life and death was thin, and that spirits roamed the land. Rather than being scary, this was thought to be a good thing, as spirits of lost loved ones were remembered and celebrated. Many families set an extra place at the table, and lit candles to light the path for any members who had passed away. Food offerings were left on doorsteps, and sacred fires were lit on hill tops as beacons of hope and light. The practice of throwing stones into the fire was carried out. These stones were left until morning, when they were fished out. If the stone was in a good condition, this meant that the person who had thrown it would be blessed for the following year. The idea of fairy spirits was also common, and it was believed that during this time fairies could step over into our world. Samhain was adopted by the Christian Church and turned into All Hallows' Eve, which eventually developed into the more popular festival of Halloween. You can still see links between the old and new festivals. For example, the idea of the pumpkin lantern comes from an old Celtic tale about a farmer called Jack who tricked the devil out of his soul so many times that when he eventually entered the underworld, the devil wouldn't let him through the gates. Instead he gave him an old turnip and a piece of burning coal which Jack used to make a lantern to light his way.

## Pumpkin power

Making pumpkin lanterns is great fun, and something you can do in well-supervised groups with children, providing you have enough helping hands. However, if that's not possible, you can still make pumpkin lanterns using card and orange tissue paper. Cut the card into the shape of a pumpkin, and cut out shapes for the eyes and mouth. As you do this, talk about the shapes you're using and why. Screw up tiny bits of orange tissue paper to make the flames and tape them on the inside. You can also make paper chains of pumpkins using card and hang flames from the ceiling by taping small bits of tissue paper to string. This is something even small children can do, as they will enjoy the action of screwing up their hands and fingers and playing with the tissue paper.

Use this session as an opportunity to talk about Halloween, and ask the children to name all the things they associate with this festival. With older children you can go on to explain that Halloween was a time when our ancestors would light fires and think of their loved ones.

## Top tip

Take the ancient tradition of throwing the stone into the fire, and turn it into a party game for all ages. Take a huge pot or box, and together have a go at decorating it so it looks like a witch's cauldron. Next get the children to make their stones using coloured paper, or buttons. To introduce the game, pretend you're a witch and get the children to chant a magical rhyme with you. Something like, 'Hocus pocus hear my spell, fill my cauldron, fill it well. I wave my wand and count to three. Hocus pocus chant with me!'

Let them take turns to throw the stone into the cauldron, each time counting how many stones are in there and repeating the rhyme. When everyone has had a go, remove the stones and count them up. Then move the cauldron further away to make it more difficult. With smaller groups you can let them take turns to become the witch and cast a Halloween spell. This provides the opportunity for some storytelling around the cauldron. Pick out your favourite picture books which feature witches, ghosts and ghouls and finish the session by reading a tale.

# Navratri

This festival, which takes place at the beginning of October (sometimes it starts in September), is one of the biggest and most significant of the Hindu calendar. The name means 'nine nights', the length of time dedicated to the celebration. It represents the triumph of good over evil and is also known as Durga Puju.

Durga is a mother goddess. She is incredibly powerful, and most famous for destroying the demon Mahishasura in an almighty battle which lasted nine days and nights. Because of this, the aspect of motherhood is celebrated at this time of year, and in particular how this relates to God. Families are encouraged to get together over the nine-day period and give thanks. Women, in particular, are encouraged to sew nine different types of seed in small pots over the nine days as an offering to the goddess. This ritual helps to ensure a good harvest for the coming year.

Navratri is thought to be one of the best times to begin new ventures, and prayers and blessings are made for prosperity and success. Festivities include great feasts and dances, where huge idols of the mother goddess are worshipped. The women dress up in their best clothes, and spend time buying new outfits, and wear gold jewellery at the nightly events. In some parts of India earthen pots are filled with water, and lamps are lit. This symbolises the divine power of the goddess. Other rituals include decorating plates in honour of the goddess.

## *Plant pot fun*

Take the tradition of planting seeds, and turn it into a session about new growth. Invest in small pots and lots of soil, and ask the children to fill the pots. Very small children will enjoy experimenting with the feel of the soil on their fingers, and you can help them pat it into the pot ready for planting. Encourage them to think about how much soil they will need, and to play with it by scooping out shapes and adding it bit by bit. This gives them a sense of space and measure and they will learn to

use their own judgement. Once the pots are full, ask them to make a hole in the centre. Again, let them have fun with this, and experiment by sticking their fingers in the soil and making different-sized holes. Finally, help them plant the seeds, covering with soil and watering. Talk about what happens next, how the seed will start to grow and push through the earth.

To finish you might want them to draw a picture of their plant in full bloom. What will it look like? What colour will it be? How big will it grow? Perhaps it's a magic plant, like a bean stalk?

## Top tip

Encourage older children to use their imagination and take the next step by creating a short story of the life of their seed. What happens if it grows and grows, and stretches up into the sky? Does it find another world in the clouds, and if so, who lives there? Perhaps it makes friends with the insects that land on it. Or maybe a fairy comes along and makes it her home. Ask them to draw out a storyboard of the seed's adventures, which they can then share with the rest of the group.

## Parent fun

Get families involved by distributing packets of seeds and asking them to plant them together at home. Encourage them to keep a record of the plant's progress, by taking pictures, which they can show the rest of the group.

## Picture plates

Take inspiration from one of the most popular rituals at Navratri, and have a go at plate decorating. Invest in paper plates, and ask the children to think of a design or picture that they'd like to draw on their plate. Help them to plan this out on paper first. They might want to draw colourful patterns, or have a go at creating a scene of a story. Older children could take this a step further and create a rhyme to go with their plate, which they can write on the reverse side. Or if they prefer, they could use a series of plates to tell a story of their choice. This is lots of fun, because once the plates are finished, you can use them in a game. Ask the children to sit around a table, and to take turns in telling their piece of the tale using the plate to illustrate the narrative.

If you have the time you might want to extend this activity and ask them to design an entire tea set, with a range of plates and cups. Once the plates have dried, make use of them and throw a tea party to celebrate!

# Development matters covered

Below you will find a list of key development matters covered in the activities above.

## Physical development

### Moving and handling

#### 8–20 months

- Picks up small objects between thumb and fingers.
- Enjoys the sensory experience of making marks in damp sand, paste or paint.

#### 16–26 months

- Beginning to balance blocks to build a small tower.
- Makes connections between their movement and the marks they make.

#### 30–50 months

- Draws lines and circles using gross motor movements.
- Uses one-handed tools and equipment, e.g. makes snips in paper with child scissors.

#### 40–60 months

- Uses simple tools to effect changes to materials.
- Handles tools, objects, construction and malleable materials safely and with increasing control.

## Mathematics

### Numbers

#### 8–20 months

- Develops an awareness of number names through their enjoyment of action rhymes and songs that relate to their experience of numbers.

#### 22–36 months

- Recites some number names in sequence.

- Knows that a group of things changes in quantity when something is added or taken away.

## 30–50 months

- Uses some number names and number language spontaneously.
- Uses some number names accurately in play.
- Recites numbers in order to 10.

### Shape, space and measure

## 16–26 months

- Uses blocks to create their own simple structures and arrangements.

## 30–50 months

- Shows an interest in shape and space by playing with shapes or making arrangements with objects.
- Shows interest in shape by sustained construction activity or by talking about shapes or arrangements.
- Shows interest in shapes in the environment.

## Literacy

### Reading

## 30–50 months

- Enjoys rhyming and rhythmic activities.
- Shows awareness of rhyme and alliteration.

## 40–60 months

- Continues a rhyming string.
- Hears and says the initial sound in words

# 🍃 *Understanding the world*

## *The world*

## 22–36 months

- Notices detailed features of objects in their environment.

## 30–50 months

- Comments and asks questions about aspects of their familiar world such as the place where they live or the natural world.
- Can talk about some of the things they have observed such as plants, animals, natural and found objects.

Development Matters in the Early Years Foundation Stage (EYFS): © Crown copyright 2012.

# 11 | November

It's only when we are surrounded by darkness that we see the light. Without the dark, the light would not shine as bright. During this month the nights draw in and a veil of darkness settles on the land. But despite the cold days and gloomy nights, it's a time of celebration, of fiery warmth and dazzling light. Most of the celebrations and festivals this month use light to their advantage, illuminating the world with knowledge, joy and abundance. Take inspiration from this in your activities and build in some light and dark. Celebrate the good things in life and rejoice in the darkness. Go for gold, and all things that glitter and bring some warmth into the classroom whilst helping the children feel empowered.

## Bonfire night – 5th November

Bonfire night marks the failed gunpowder plot, a plan hatched by Guy Fawkes. Guy's intention was to blow up the Houses of Parliament. The plot was foiled at some point between the 4th and 5th of November 1605. To commemorate this, fires were burned, and effigies of Guy were placed on top. More recently fireworks have been added to the celebrations.

### Flame dance

Gathering around a fire is something our ancestors have been doing for decades to celebrate a number of events and festivals. In fact this type of ritual is popular throughout the world with many different cultures. Fire is a symbol of action and movement. It's often considered a cleansing force, and used in rituals to give thanks, release the past and embrace the cycle of life. Use it today to show younger children

the difference between light and dark. Build a make-believe fire in the middle of your classroom, using materials you have to hand. Think about how you will create the colour and glow of the flames. Think about the kind of noise that you might hear as you gather around a roaring fire and encourage the children to make these sounds. Think about what you might throw into the fire, and ask everyone to draw a picture or write a word to represent a wish or dream. For example, if they would like a pet cat, they might draw a picture of a cat, or if they would like to go to the seaside they might draw a bucket and spade, or write the word 'sea' on the paper. Place a waste paper bin in the centre of your makeshift fire and ask them to take turns, make a wish out loud and throw their paper in the bin. Take this a step further by creating a short rhyme that you can chant together as you move around the fire. Something simple like, 'As the flames reach higher and higher, we feel the heat of this fire. We walk in a circle, we chant this rhyme, we wave and clap our hands in time. Red, orange, yellow, gold, these are the colours the flames glow!'

## Top tip

Encourage the children to pretend they are the flames of the fire. Ask them to think about different ways of moving. Go from crouching down low as the flames are just ignited, and then take them on a journey as they grow, and twist and wave until they are stretched on their tiptoes reaching for the sky.

# Diwali

This Hindu festival usually falls in November, sometimes October, depending on how the Hindu calendar relates to the western calendar. It's known as the festival of lights and it extends over five days. A riot of colour and energy, there are fireworks, parties and lots of sweet treats, making this a popular event with children. In essence, Diwali is about good conquering evil, it symbolises light over darkness and there is a general feeling of goodwill to all men. Traditionally it was a time to celebrate and give thanks for a good harvest. During the festival people dress up in their best clothes, spring clean their home and decorate it with lamps and candles. The lamps they use are called divas, the idea being that they light the path for the goddess Lakshmi, so that she can make her way into every home and place of work. Doors and windows are often left open for this purpose, and many people decorate their home with lotus flowers, as these are also associated with the goddess. Lakshmi is the goddess of wealth, and many people create an altar at this time and decorate it with money and images of wealth, to attract good fortune. It's also believed to be a good time to start a new business.

## Money tree

Imagine you had your own money tree growing in the centre of the room. What would it look like? Would it have notes, and gold coins instead of leaves? What colour would it be? Perhaps it would grow out of a pot of gold, and be surrounded by lots of gifts and presents. How would you decorate it? Explain to the group that you are going to build a money tree for the goddess Lakshmi and to celebrate Diwali. Sketch an outline on a giant piece of paper, or alternatively use several separate pieces that you can put together to form the tree and fill the classroom. Give each group part of the tree to colour in and decorate. Ask them to make gold coins and lanterns that they can stick on to the tree, and turn it into a giant collage that you can eventually hang on the wall. Be creative and get the group to hunt for materials that they can use to represent the bark and the leaves. For example, you might be able to collect twigs from outside that you can stick together to form the bark. Encourage them to look at trees growing for inspiration. Get them thinking about words associated with trees, and ask them to describe what they see. Use this as an excuse to get to grips with nature, and encourage them to feel the bark, to hug its trunk, and to think about all the animals that might live in the tree.

## Bird's-eye view

This follow-on activity is a perfect way to stretch the imagination and works well with older children. Get them to imagine that they are a tree. Explain that they have lived on the earth for hundreds of years and that they have seen many things. Ask them to imagine what this is like. What do they see when they look at their surroundings? They might think that it's the same picture every day, but encourage them to think about the changing seasons and how this might affect their outlook. Use a storyboard to illustrate the changes through the year, and get them to draw the view in spring, summer, autumn and winter. Encourage them to use descriptive words and sentences to describe the sequence of events.

# Shichigosan (7-5-3) festival – usually celebrated on 15th November

This festival, based on the specific ages of the children involved, is a time to give thanks for a healthy life. Parents take boys aged three and five years old and girls of three and seven to give thanks to the gods for their life. This is an auspicious occasion, and the children will often dress up in traditional costume or their best clothes.

## How old am I?

As this festival is about the age of the children involved, it's a great excuse for a numbers game that you can do with very young children. Sit them in a circle and begin with a simple rhyming chant, something like 'How old am I? Let's clap and count the numbers out. How old am I?' Go around the circle repeating the chant each time, and then getting the children to clap out their ages together. So you might respond to the chant by saying, 'Lisa is three. Let's clap and count the numbers out. Lisa is three.' Then clap three times together. Once you've been around the group and clapped out everyone's age, you can introduce a guessing element to the game, by going back to different children within the group and asking, 'How old is Lisa? Let's clap and count the numbers out. How old is Lisa?'

## Numbers and words

Take this a step further, and get the children to colour and decorate giant numbers which represent their age. Encourage them to think of their favourite things and include them in the picture. For example, if Lisa likes the colour orange, flowers and teddy bears, then she might want to include lots of orange flowery patterns in a giant number three, and also draw a teddy bear next to it. With older children you can ask them to decorate the numbers and then come up with words for the things they like doing and have a go at writing them on the page. When they've finished they will have a number for how old they are and a picture, with lots of key words describing all the things they enjoy. You can use this in another game where you pull out a picture and get the children to guess who drew it, by looking at their age, and the things they like. Encourage interaction by asking questions, and with each picture clap out the numbers together.

# St Andrew's Day – 30th November

Patron saint of Scotland, St Andrew was thought to be Jesus Christ's first disciple. A strong character, Andrew came from a family of fishermen. He first met John the Baptist on the banks of Jordan, and later became a follower of Jesus. His exploits include travelling to Asia Minor and the Black Sea, and battling his way through a forest in Greece filled with wolves, bears and tigers. Andrew was crucified, and at his own request the cross was set diagonally as he didn't feel worthy enough to be crucified upright like Christ. His bones were thought to have come to St Andrews in Scotland around 732 AD, by the Bishop of Hexham. Traditionally St Andrew's Day was a time for great feasting. The people would catch rabbits and squirrels for the pot, and throw a party. Today it is celebrated with music, Scottish dancing, storytelling and poetry.

## Fishing fun

Together you're going to create a collage of the sea, which will include lots of different-coloured fish, a fishing net and some fishermen to commemorate Andrew's life. Start by telling a very short story or poem about Andrew's life. Explain that you are going to imagine what it would be like to be a fisherman. Split the class into smaller groups and give them a designated area of the picture to work on. Encourage them to think about colour and texture, and to use lots of different materials to build up the picture. Get creative by adding movement, so for example you might cut out and create fish that you can move along the waves, and position in different places in the picture. If you have the space, you can turn your entire classroom into the ocean. Use pictures to decorate the walls, and drape material, cushions and mats to depict the seabed around the room. When you've finished use this space for some 'fishy' storytelling.

Start with something simple like a magical tale about an underwater world. Set the scene and talk about the different creatures that live there. Make this fun by having a storytelling fish; this can be a picture or a clay model that you pass around the group. When the storytelling fish lands in your hands you have to add something to the story. Younger children might not be able to tell the story, but they can join in by adding sound and movement. So encourage them to make noise when it's their turn.

# Development matters covered

Below you will find a list of key development matters covered in the activities above.

## Personal, social and emotional development

### Making relationships

22–36 months

- Interested in others' play and starting to join in.
- Seeks out others to share experiences.

## 30–50 months

- Can play in a group, extending and elaborating play ideas, e.g. building up a role-play activity with other children.
- Initiates play, offering cues to peers to join them.
- Keeps play going by responding to what others are saying or doing.
- Demonstrates friendly behaviour, initiating conversations and forming good relationships with peers and familiar adults.

### Self-confidence and self-awareness

## 30–50 months

- Can select and use activities and resources with help.

# Communication and language

### Listening and attention

## 8–20 months

- Has a strong exploratory impulse.
- Concentrates intently on an object or activity of own choosing for short periods.

## 16–26 months

- Listens to and enjoys rhythmic patterns in rhymes and stories.
- Enjoys rhymes and demonstrates listening by trying to join in with actions or vocalisation.

## 22–36 months

- Listens with interest to the noises adults make when they read stories.
- Shows interest in play with sounds, songs and rhymes.

## 30–50 months

- Listens to others one to one or in small groups, when conversation interests them.
- Joins in with repeated refrains and anticipates key events and phrases in rhymes and stories.

- Is able to follow directions (if not intently focused on own choice of activity).
- Listens to stories with increasing attention and recall.

## Understanding

### 16–26 months

- Understands simple sentences, e.g. 'Throw the ball.'

### 22–36 months

- Understands more complex sentences, e.g. 'Put your toys away and then we'll read a book.'
- Understands 'who', 'what', 'where' in simple questions, e.g. Who's that/who can? What's that? Where is . . .?

### 30–50 months

- Understands use of objects, e.g. 'What do we use to cut things?'
- Responds to simple instructions, e.g. to get or put away an object.
- Beginning to understand 'why' and 'how' questions.

### 40–60 months

- Able to follow a story without pictures or props.
- Listens and responds to ideas expressed by others in conversation or discussion.

## Speaking

### 8–20 months

- Frequently imitates words and sounds.
- Enjoys babbling and increasingly experiments with using sounds and words to communicate for a range of purposes, e.g. teddy, more, no, bye-bye.
- Uses sounds in play, e.g. 'brrrm' for toy car.
- Uses single words.

### 16–26 months

- Uses different types of everyday words (nouns, verbs and adjectives, e.g. banana, go, sleep, hot).
- Beginning to ask simple questions.

## 22–36 months

- Learns new words very rapidly and is able to use them in communicating.
- Uses gestures, sometimes with limited talk, e.g. reaches toward toy, saying 'I have it'.
- Uses a variety of questions, e.g. what, where, who.
- Uses simple sentences, e.g. 'Mummy gonna work.'
- Uses language as a powerful means of widening contacts, sharing feelings, experiences and thoughts.
- Holds a conversation, jumping from topic to topic.

## 30–50 months

- Beginning to use more complex sentences to link thoughts, e.g. using 'and' and 'because'.
- Uses talk to connect ideas, explain what is happening and anticipate what might happen next, recall and relive past experiences.
- Questions why things happen and gives explanations. Asks e.g. who, what, when, how.
- Builds up vocabulary that reflects the breadth of their experiences.
- Uses talk in pretending that objects stand for something else in play, e.g. 'This box is my castle'.

## 40–60 months

- Uses language to imagine and recreate roles and experiences in play situations.
- Introduces a storyline or narrative into their play.
- Extends vocabulary, especially by grouping and naming, exploring the meaning and sounds of new words.

## *Physical development*

### *Moving and handling*

### 8–20 months

- Crawls, bottom shuffles or rolls continuously to move around.
- Picks up small objects between thumb and fingers.
- Enjoys the sensory experience of making marks in damp sand, paste or paint.

- Holds pen or crayon using a whole hand (palmar) grasp and makes random marks with different strokes.

## 16–26 months

- Makes connections between their movement and the marks they make.

## 22–36 months

- Shows control in holding and using jugs to pour, hammers, books and mark-making tools.
- Squats with steadiness to rest or play with object on the ground, and rises to feet without using hands.
- Beginning to use three fingers (tripod grip) to hold writing tools.
- Imitates drawing simple shapes such as circles and lines.

## 30–50 months

- Draws lines and circles using gross motor movements.
- Uses one-handed tools and equipment, e.g. makes snips in paper with child scissors.
- Moves freely and with pleasure and confidence in a range of ways, such as slithering, shuffling, rolling, crawling, walking, running, jumping, skipping, sliding and hopping.

## 40–60 months

- Uses simple tools to effect changes to materials.
- Handles tools, objects, construction and malleable materials safely and with increasing control.
- Experiments with different ways of moving.

# Literacy

## Reading

## 22–36 months

- Has some favourite stories, rhymes, songs, poems or jingles.
- Repeats words or phrases from familiar stories.

## 30–50 months

- Enjoys rhyming and rhythmic activities.
- Shows awareness of rhyme and alliteration.
- Listens to and joins in with stories and poems, one to one and also in small groups.
- Joins in with repeated refrains and anticipates key events and phrases in rhymes and stories.
- Beginning to be aware of the way stories are structured.
- Suggests how the story might end.
- Listens to stories with increasing attention and recall.
- Describes main story settings, events and principal characters.

## 40–60 months

- Uses vocabulary and forms of speech that are increasingly influenced by their experiences of books.
- Continues a rhyming string.
- Hears and says the initial sound in words.

### Writing

## 30–50 months

- Sometimes gives meaning to marks as they draw and paint.

## 40–60 months

- Gives meaning to marks they make as they draw, write and paint.
- Begins to break the flow of speech into words.
- Continues a rhyming string.

## Mathematics

### Numbers

## 8–20 months

- Develops an awareness of number names through their enjoyment of action rhymes and songs that relate to their experience of numbers.

## 22–36 months

- Recites some number names in sequence.
- Creates and experiments with symbols and marks representing ideas of number.
- Begins to make comparisons between quantities.

## 30–50 months

- Uses some number names and number language spontaneously.
- Uses some number names accurately in play.
- Recites numbers in order to 10.
- Knows that numbers identify how many objects are in a set.
- Beginning to represent numbers using fingers, marks on paper or pictures.
- Sometimes matches numeral and quantity correctly.

## 40–60 months

- Recognises some numerals of personal significance.
- Recognises numerals 1 to 5.
- Counts up to three or four objects by saying one number name for each item.

## *Shape, space and measure*

## 22–36 months

- Notices simple shapes and patterns in pictures.

## 30–50 months

- Shows an interest in shape and space by playing with shapes or making arrangements with objects.
- Shows interest in shapes in the environment.
- Uses shapes appropriately for tasks.
- Beginning to talk about the shapes of everyday objects, e.g. 'round' and 'tall'.

## 40–60 months

- Uses familiar objects and common shapes to create and recreate patterns and build models.

# Understanding the world

## People and communities

### 16–26 months

- Is curious about people and shows interest in stories about themselves and their family.
- Enjoys pictures and stories about themselves, their families and other people.

### 22–36 months

- Learns that they have similarities and differences that connect them to, and distinguish them from, others.

### 30–50 months

- Remembers and talks about significant events in their own experience.
- Recognises and describes special times or events for family or friends.

## The world

### 16–26 months

- Explores objects by linking together different approaches: shaking, hitting, looking, feeling, tasting, mouthing, pulling, turning and poking.
- Remembers where objects belong.
- Matches parts of objects that fit together, e.g. puts lid on teapot.

### 22–36 months

- Notices detailed features of objects in their environment.

### 30–50 months

- Comments and asks questions about aspects of their familiar world such as the place where they live or the natural world.
- Can talk about some of the things they have observed such as plants, animals, natural and found objects.
- Shows care and concern for living things and the environment.

# 🎵 *Expressive arts and design*

## *Exploring and using media and materials*

### 8–20 months

- Imitates and improvises actions they have observed, e.g. clapping or waving.
- Begins to move to music, listen to or join in rhymes or songs.
- Notices and is interested in the effects of making movements which leave marks.
- Explores and experiments with a range of media through sensory exploration, and using whole body.
- Moves whole body to enjoyable sounds, such as music or a regular beat.

### 22–36 months

- Experiments with blocks, colours and marks.
- Creates sounds by banging, shaking, tapping or blowing.

### 30–50 months

- Enjoys joining in with dancing and ring games.
- Imitates movement in response to music.
- Beginning to be interested in and describe the texture of things.
- Beginning to move rhythmically.
- Understands that they can use lines to enclose a space, and then begins to use these shapes to represent objects.
- Uses various construction materials.
- Beginning to construct, stacking blocks vertically and horizontally, making enclosures and creating spaces.
- Joins construction pieces together to build and balance.
- Realises tools can be used for a purpose.

### 40–60 months

- Explores what happens when they mix colours.
- Experiments to create different textures.
- Manipulates materials to achieve a planned effect.
- Constructs with a purpose in mind, using a variety of resources.

- Uses simple tools and techniques competently and appropriately.
- Selects tools and techniques needed to shape, assemble and join materials they are using.

## Being imaginative

### 16–26 months

- Expresses self through physical action and sound.
- Pretends that one object represents another, especially when objects have characteristics in common.

### 22–36 months

- Beginning to make-believe by pretending.

### 30–50 months

- Uses available resources to create props to support role-play.
- Captures experiences and responses with a range of media, such as music, dance and paint and other materials or words.
- Engages in imaginative role-play based on own first-hand experiences.
- Builds stories around toys, e.g. farm animals needing rescue from an armchair 'cliff'.
- Uses available resources to create props to support role-play.

### 40–60 months

- Chooses particular colours to use for a purpose.
- Plays alongside other children who are engaged in the same theme.
- Plays cooperatively as part of a group to develop and act out a narrative.
- Introduces a storyline or narrative into their play.
- Creates simple representations of events, people and objects.

Development Matters in the Early Years Foundation Stage (EYFS): © Crown copyright 2012.

# 12 | December

A magical month, December lends itself to celebration. Take inspiration from the changing landscape and think about how our ancestors might have marked this transition. Trees feature in many festivals. They represent an aspect of nature that is timeless and they also reflect the changes in the seasons in a visual way. They're a solid skeletal structure, from which you can build a picture or a story and give it different strands. Think about the way the branches grow and stretch and how the roots also spread out to anchor the tree to the earth. Use this as a way to plan your activities, starting with the bare bones of an idea and building upon this by adding colour and texture. Most importantly, have fun and encourage the children to see and experience the wonder all around them!

## Bodhi Day – 8th December

Bodhi Day, also called the day of enlightenment, is celebrated by Buddhists around the world. It marks the eight days that Buddha sat fasting and meditating beneath the Bodhi tree.

In particular, it celebrates the final day when enlightenment came, and Buddha made several realisations, which would become the core principles of Buddhism. On this day Buddhists sit and meditate, often lighting candles and giving thanks for Buddha's enlightenment. They may eat a meal of rice and milk, which is believed to be the first meal that Buddha had once he'd emerged from the tree. Homes are decorated with lights and candles, and trees are also decorated with lanterns and beads.

## Leaf ritual

The leaves of the sacred Bodhi tree are heart-shaped, and as the tree is a symbol of enlightenment, its leaves have a special power too. Before the session, sketch and cut out a number of large heart-shaped leaves, at least one for every child in the group. Start by telling the children the story of the Bodhi tree, and describe what it might have looked like and how it pro-tected Buddha as he sat beneath its branches. Next give them a leaf cutting and ask them to decorate the leaf and draw pictures of things that they love in the space provided. Very young children will enjoy colouring in the leaf and using it to flap and wave, whilst older children can use key words and pictures to decorate the shape. Sketch out the skeletal trunk of a tree with branches on a large sheet of paper and pin on the wall. Now ask each child to stick his or her leaf somewhere on the tree until all the branches are full and everyone has taken their turn. Older children can take the floor and explain what they have drawn and why, before adding their leaf to the picture.

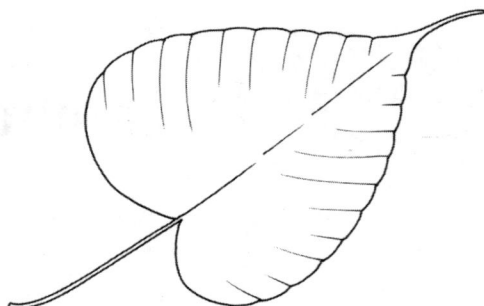

### Top tip

Use the tree as a notice board, so every week clear away the 'used' leaves (you can keep them in a memory box to provide inspiration for future sessions) and give out blank ones that the children can decorate or write upon. They can use the leaves to tell stories or rhymes, or just for drawing pictures. Take this a step further and give them a theme every week. So, for example, if your theme is 'rainy days', then you might ask the children to draw pictures of a rainy day, come up with rhymes or write key words to describe the rain on the leaves, then you can decorate the tree and even add a rain cloud above it. This would work with all the seasons and different types of weather.

# The winter solstice – 21st December

This pagan festival marks the arrival of the shortest day of the year, and was celebrated long before Christianity. It embraces the coming of winter and the cycles of life. The druids, in particular, commemorated this time of year. They believed that the oak tree was sacred, and would take cuttings of mistletoe from it and use it in their rituals. They believed that the plant had protective qualities and could bring blessings and good fortune. They also started the tradition of the yule log. The log was lit from the embers of the log from the previous year to represent the continuing cycle of life. It was a symbol of light, and burning it was thought to bring good fortune for the coming year.

## Mistletoe magic

If you can't get hold of real mistletoe, have a go at making your own using brown and green clay, and white beads for the berries. This is a great starter activity and gets everyone in the festive mood. Next decorate the room with mistletoe, and make sure you hide it in lots of different places. Split the group into pairs and ask them to go on a mistletoe hunt. They must try and find as many pieces as they can to win the game! If you have the opportunity, you could take this game outside, and create a mistletoe trail.

# Christmas Day – 25th December

This festival celebrates the birth of Christ and tells the story of how he was born in a manger, with all the animals around him. Marked as one of the most important Christian celebrations, it's a time when gifts are given, and if children have been good, then Santa will visit.

## Nativity play

Start by getting the children to think about all the characters involved in the nativity story. So tell the tale, and then talk about all the various people involved. Ask them to pick a character and draw a picture of them. Encourage them to think about all the characters, including the animals in the stable and the inn-keeper. Next sit in a circle and begin a storytelling rhyme using sound and movement. So you might say, 'Knock knock knock on the stable door [make the knocking sound together]. Who could it be? Shall we see?'

Then go around the circle and encourage the children to suggest who might be at the stable door. They can use their pictures as prompts, or come up with new characters. If you include animals, remember to include any sounds they might make.

**Top tip**

Give older children the chance to come up with a story from the perspective of the character they have chosen. Give them a prompt by saying, 'I remember the night that Jesus was born . . .' Then encourage them to write or speak a few sentences and describe what happened next. What did they see or do, and how did they feel? Encourage them to flesh this out with a storyboard, so they have a series of pictures and words to describe their version of events.

## Saturnalia – 17th December

Saturnalia is a Roman festival that lasted for several days, beginning on the 17th December. It was a time for celebrating the cycles of life and the rebirth of the year. The Romans treated it as a huge knees-up and an excuse to make merry and have lots of fun. It was a time when the tables were turned, and masters would dress as servants and wait upon them, serving them food and seeing to their every need. Men would also dress as women, and vice versa. Feasts were held, and homes were decorated with candles.

### Mirror image

Split the group into pairs of roughly the same age group. They're going to pretend that they're looking through a mirror. One child is the reflection and must copy everything the other child, the master, does in order to look like them. Start with simple activities like waving, tapping hands and feet and then move on to more complicated gestures and signs. Encourage the children to move around. Wherever child number one goes, child number two must follow and copy their actions. Make sure that you allow them to reverse roles so that each child gets a turn at being the master and creating the movements. Try this with larger groups, and finish by doing it together to music in one big group. Let the children take it in turns to take the spotlight and control the movements of the entire class.

### Clown capers

The Romans were known for their ability to have fun and enjoyed playing the fool. Embrace this by having a 'clowning' session. Encourage the children to dress up in silly clothes and get into the spirit of the occasion. Bring in face paint, so that they can experiment with different looks. Get them laughing in a group. Start with a 'ho ho ho' sound and then build up in speed and volume. Sway forwards and back and encourage them to go for a belly laugh. Think about the way clowns move and why this is funny. For example, they might want to roll, or bend, or jump up and down.

Ask older children to consider what makes them laugh and why? Encourage them to come up with a mini clowning routine that they can perform to the rest of the group.

# Development matters covered

Below you will find a list of key development matters covered in the activities above.

## Personal, social and emotional development

### Making relationships

#### 22–36 months

- Interested in others' play and starting to join in.
- Seeks out others to share experiences.

#### 30–50 months

- Can play in a group, extending and elaborating play ideas, e.g. building up a role-play activity with other children.
- Initiates play, offering cues to peers to join them.
- Keeps play going by responding to what others are saying or doing.
- Demonstrates friendly behaviour, initiating conversations and forming good relationships with peers and familiar adults.

### Self-confidence and self-awareness

#### 16–26 months

- Gradually able to engage in pretend play with toys (supports child to understand their own thinking may be different from others').

#### 30–50 months

- Can select and use activities and resources with help.
- Confident to talk to other children when playing, and will communicate freely about own home and community.

# 💬 Communication and language

## Listening and attention

### 8–20 months

- Has a strong exploratory impulse.
- Concentrates intently on an object or activity of own choosing for short periods.

### 16–26 months

- Listens to and enjoys rhythmic patterns in rhymes and stories.
- Enjoys rhymes and demonstrates listening by trying to join in with actions or vocalisation.

### 22–36 months

- Listens with interest to the noises adults make when they read stories.
- Shows interest in play with sounds, songs and rhymes.

### 30–50 months

- Listens to others one to one or in small groups, when conversation interests them.
- Joins in with repeated refrains and anticipates key events and phrases in rhymes and stories.
- Is able to follow directions (if not intently focused on own choice of activity).
- Listens to stories with increasing attention and recall.

## Understanding

### 8–20 months

- Developing the ability to follow others' body language, including pointing and gesture.

### 16–26 months

- Understands simple sentences, e.g. 'Throw the ball.'

### 22–36 months

- Understands more complex sentences, e.g. 'Put your toys away and then we'll read a book.'

- Understands 'who', 'what', 'where' in simple questions, e.g. Who's that/who can? What's that? Where is . . .?
- Developing understanding of simple concepts, e.g. big/little.

## 30–50 months

- Understands use of objects, e.g. 'What do we use to cut things?'
- Responds to simple instructions, e.g. to get or put away an object.
- Beginning to understand 'why' and 'how' questions.

## 40–60 months

- Able to follow a story without pictures or props.
- Listens and responds to ideas expressed by others in conversation or discussion.

### Speaking

## 8–20 months

- Frequently imitates words and sounds.
- Enjoys babbling and increasingly experiments with using sounds and words to communicate for a range of purposes, e.g. teddy, more, no, bye-bye.
- Uses sounds in play, e.g. 'brrrm' for toy car.
- Uses single words.

## 16–26 months

- Uses different types of everyday words (nouns, verbs and adjectives, e.g. banana, go, sleep, hot).
- Beginning to ask simple questions.
- Beginning to put two words together, e.g. 'want ball', 'more juice'.

## 22–36 months

- Learns new words very rapidly and is able to use them in communicating.
- Uses a variety of questions, e.g. what, where, who.
- Uses simple sentences, e.g. 'Mummy gonna work.'
- Uses language as a powerful means of widening contacts, sharing feelings, experiences and thoughts.
- Holds a conversation, jumping from topic to topic.

## 30–50 months

- Beginning to use more complex sentences to link thoughts, e.g. using 'and' and 'because'.
- Uses talk to connect ideas, explain what is happening and anticipate what might happen next, recall and relive past experiences.
- Questions why things happen and gives explanations. Asks e.g. who, what, when, how.
- Builds up vocabulary that reflects the breadth of their experiences.
- Uses talk in pretending that objects stand for something else in play, e.g. 'This box is my castle'.

## 40–60 months

- Uses language to imagine and recreate roles and experiences in play situations.
- Introduces a storyline or narrative into their play.
- Extends vocabulary, especially by grouping and naming, exploring the meaning and sounds of new words.
- Uses talk to organise, sequence and clarify thinking, ideas, feelings and events.

## *Physical development*

### *Moving and handling*

#### 8–20 months

- Crawls, bottom shuffles or rolls continuously to move around.
- Picks up small objects between thumb and fingers.
- Enjoys the sensory experience of making marks in damp sand, paste or paint.
- Holds pen or crayon using a whole hand (palmar) grasp and makes random marks with different strokes.
- Sits unsupported on the floor.

#### 16–26 months

- Makes connections between their movement and the marks they make.

#### 22–36 months

- Shows control in holding and using jugs to pour, hammers, books and mark-making tools.

- Squats with steadiness to rest or play with object on the ground, and rises to feet without using hands.
- Beginning to use three fingers (tripod grip) to hold writing tools.
- Imitates drawing simple shapes such as circles and lines.

## 30–50 months

- Draws lines and circles using gross motor movements.
- Uses one-handed tools and equipment, e.g. makes snips in paper with child scissors.
- Moves freely and with pleasure and confidence in a range of ways, such as slithering, shuffling, rolling, crawling, walking, running, jumping, skipping, sliding and hopping.
- Can stand momentarily on one foot when shown.

## 40–60 months

- Uses simple tools to effect changes to materials.
- Handles tools, objects, construction and malleable materials safely and with increasing control.
- Travels with confidence and skill around, under, over and through balancing and climbing equipment.
- Experiments with different ways of moving.

# Literacy

## Reading

### 22–36 months

- Has some favourite stories, rhymes, songs, poems or jingles.
- Repeats words or phrases from familiar stories.

### 30–50 months

- Enjoys rhyming and rhythmic activities.
- Shows awareness of rhyme and alliteration.
- Listens to and joins in with stories and poems, one to one and also in small groups.
- Joins in with repeated refrains and anticipates key events and phrases in rhymes and stories.

- Beginning to be aware of the way stories are structured.
- Suggests how the story might end.
- Listens to stories with increasing attention and recall.
- Describes main story settings, events and principal characters.

## 40–60 months

- Uses vocabulary and forms of speech that are increasingly influenced by their experiences of books.
- Continues a rhyming string.
- Hears and says the initial sound in words.

### Writing

## 30–50 months

- Sometimes gives meaning to marks as they draw and paint.

## 40–60 months

- Gives meaning to marks they make as they draw, write and paint.
- Begins to break the flow of speech into words.
- Continues a rhyming string.

## Mathematics

### Shape, space and measure

## 22–36 months

- Notices simple shapes and patterns in pictures.

## 30–50 months

- Shows an interest in shape and space by playing with shapes or making arrangements with objects.
- Shows interest in shapes in the environment.
- Uses shapes appropriately for tasks.
- Beginning to talk about the shapes of everyday objects, e.g. 'round' and 'tall'.

## 40–60 months

- Uses familiar objects and common shapes to create and recreate patterns and build models.

## Understanding the world

### People and communities

#### 16–26 months

- Is curious about people and shows interest in stories about themselves and their family.
- Enjoys pictures and stories about themselves, their families and other people.

#### 22–36 months

- Learns that they have similarities and differences that connect them to, and distinguish them from, others.

#### 30–50 months

- Remembers and talks about significant events in their own experience.
- Recognises and describes special times or events for family or friends.

### The world

#### 8–20 months

- Watches toy being hidden and tries to find it.
- Looks for dropped objects.

#### 16–26 months

- Explores objects by linking together different approaches: shaking, hitting, looking, feeling, tasting, mouthing, pulling, turning and poking.
- Remembers where objects belong.
- Matches parts of objects that fit together, e.g. puts lid on teapot.

#### 22–36 months

- Notices detailed features of objects in their environment.

## 30–50 months

- Comments and asks questions about aspects of their familiar world such as the place where they live or the natural world.
- Can talk about some of the things they have observed such as plants, animals, natural and found objects.
- Shows care and concern for living things and the environment.

## 🎵 *Expressive arts and design*

### *Exploring and using media and materials*

### 8–20 months

- Imitates and improvises actions they have observed, e.g. clapping or waving.
- Begins to move to music, listen to or join in rhymes or songs.
- Notices and is interested in the effects of making movements which leave marks.
- Explores and experiments with a range of media through sensory exploration, and using whole body.
- Moves whole body to enjoyable sounds, such as music or a regular beat.

### 22–36 months

- Experiments with blocks, colours and marks.
- Creates sounds by banging, shaking, tapping or blowing.

### 30–50 months

- Enjoys joining in with dancing and ring games.
- Imitates movement in response to music.
- Beginning to be interested in and describe the texture of things.
- Beginning to move rhythmically.
- Understands that they can use lines to enclose a space, and then begin to use these shapes to represent objects.
- Uses various construction materials.
- Beginning to construct, stacking blocks vertically and horizontally, making enclosures and creating spaces.
- Joins construction pieces together to build and balance.
- Realises tools can be used for a purpose.

## 40–60 months

- Explores what happens when they mix colours.
- Experiments to create different textures.
- Manipulates materials to achieve a planned effect.
- Constructs with a purpose in mind, using a variety of resources.
- Uses simple tools and techniques competently and appropriately.
- Selects tools and techniques needed to shape, assemble and join materials they are using.

### Being imaginative

## 16–26 months

- Expresses self through physical action and sound.
- Pretends that one object represents another, especially when objects have characteristics in common.

## 22–36 months

- Beginning to make-believe by pretending.

## 30–50 months

- Uses available resources to create props to support role-play.
- Captures experiences and responses with a range of media, such as music, dance and paint and other materials or words.
- Engages in imaginative role-play based on own first-hand experiences.
- Builds stories around toys, e.g. farm animals needing rescue from an armchair 'cliff'.
- Uses available resources to create props to support role-play.
- Developing preferences for forms of expression.
- Uses movement to express feelings.

## 40–60 months

- Chooses particular colours to use for a purpose.
- Plays alongside other children who are engaged in the same theme.
- Plays cooperatively as part of a group to develop and act out a narrative.

- Introduces a storyline or narrative into their play.
- Creates simple representations of events, people and objects.

Development Matters in the Early Years Foundation Stage (EYFS): © Crown copyright 2012.

# 13 | **Other ideas**

This section provides basic rituals that can be adapted to suit most festivals. These are common activities linked to celebrations, and you will be able to use these ideas as a starting point for any event.

## Circle dance

The circle is a common symbol throughout the world and appears in many different religions and spiritualities. It symbolises the ongoing nature of life, and can be used as a way of joining people together. A circle dance is something you can do with any age group. In its most basic form, it involves positioning everyone in a circle and moving either clockwise or anticlockwise. How you move is up to you, and you can tie this in with the event that you are celebrating. For example, if the festival is linked to the sun, you might think of vibrant fiery ways to move with lots of action. If on the other hand the festival is linked to the sea, you might think of more fluid ways to dance around.

### Top tip

- Be creative. Mix your circles up. Have lots of different-sized circles doing different things, in different locations. If you're limited on space, have one large circle and smaller circles positioned inside. This is a great way to help younger children understand the concept of shape and size, and how things fit together.

- Circles connect people, so use this to your advantage. Make the circle a sharing space where children can come up with ideas and suggestions relating to the festival.

- Experiment with other shapes, once you've mastered the circle. Try moving from this formation into something new, like a rectangle, square or oval. This will probably involve some tricky engineering of obstacles, and the way the children move around the room.

# Storytelling

Stories are an essential part of most religious and spiritual paths. They are a way of helping people connect, and also creating a common landscape. Most festivals will have some sort of tale or myth that can be recited or used as a starting point for creative activities.

## Top tip

- Keep it simple. Think of the story as linear and use storyboards to illustrate how it moves from one section to the next. This will help the children understand the basic structure.
- Include a point of crisis. Most tales reach a point where they can go in any direction. It is at this point that you can make the tale interactive and get the children to come up with their ideas.
- Make it real by putting them in the story. Always remember to use characters of the same age so that they can identify with them, and try and include experiences that they have already had, so they have a point of reference.
- Repetition is key. Include phrases, rhymes and words that you can repeat over and over again. This will not only hold their attention, as they will be waiting for the opportunity to join in and have some fun, but it will help them learn new vocabulary.

# Making an altar

An altar can be any kind of space or designated area that is dedicated to a particular festival. Something simple like a table in the corner of the room can easily be turned into an altar of celebration. The key is what you put on the table to make it special. Festivals tend to focus on rituals, so the creation of an altar should be seen in this way. Start by coming up with initial ideas, and then make an event of it, by inviting the children to place the objects they have either made or brought in on the altar. Play some music, chant some words and get into the spirit of the occasion.

## Top tip

- If you're dealing with a specific event or festival, think about the key themes. For example, if it's linked to the sun, then an image of the sun would make a good centre piece; if it's linked to a particular god, then you might want to incorporate drawings of this deity.

- Consider colours. Most festivals use colour in some way or have specific shades associated with them, so make sure you incorporate them into your altar.

- What is the message behind the festival? Older children might want to think about this, and come up with pictures or objects that help them identify with the meaning of the celebration.

- Remember that an altar or sacred space is personal to those who create it. If you're getting the children involved, then let them take the lead and use this space to express themselves.

## Processions

Many celebrations include processions, usually through the town, or a local place of worship. Sometimes these events are small and intimate, and sometimes they're a huge happening with everyone involved. The beauty of any kind of procession is that you can have it anywhere. On a basic level, it's about motivating the group to move, in a fashion, or to a specific pattern. How they move and the shapes they make are entirely up to you, and that's part of the fun!

## Top tip

- Processions are a great excuse to dress up, and make props. So use this opportunity and think about outfits and objects you might want to carry as part of the celebration.

- Get children moving and creating different patterns and shapes wherever possible. Remember, movement isn't just about getting on their feet. They can move in many ways, from crawling with very young children, to hopping, skipping, jumping and marching. Also think about other parts of the body and how you can get them involved.

- If you can, take your procession outside and include the environment by making it a feature of the celebration. For example, you might want to lead the procession to a tree and then dance around it in a circle.

- If you're limited for space, plot out a course in the classroom. Either outline the pattern of the procession on the floor, or use chairs and tables and navigate around them.

# Hide-and-seek games

Hide-and-seek games are popular because you can do them with large groups and they work with most ages. The key is to give the game a theme, by hiding something that links in to a festival, for example bunnies or chocolate eggs at Easter. You can also give the children a character to play or put them in a scenario that relates to the event, where they might have to find things. Take the game outside if you can, so that they can have first-hand experience of the environment. If this isn't possible, include your surroundings in the game by using props and encouraging the children to imagine the classroom as a different setting. Always start by asking what you would like them to learn from this experience. If the primary objective is to get them manoeuvring around objects, then make sure you include lots of objects for them to move around. If it's more of a word game, then leave letters dotted around the room, and encourage them to find the letters and make a word. The winner is the child who makes the most words out of the letters. Hide and seek is such a flexible game because of its simple premise; this means it's adaptable and you can get it to work for you.

## *Parent fun*

It's important to get families involved, so that the learning and creativity can continue. Look for opportunities where you can take the learning out of the classroom. If you have done something together, like planting seeds, then this is easy to transfer to the home and encourage parents to repeat the exercise. Encourage the children to share what they have done, and take home contributions, or continue creating at home. For example, if they've been drawing a picture of what they can see through their classroom window, encourage them to do the same at home, when they look out of their bedroom window. Invite parents in for special show-and-tell events, and use the range of celebrations in this book as an excuse to create your own events.